KETO COOKBOOK

AFTER 50

The Complete Ketogenic Guide, With 200 Delicious & Effective Recipes For Seniors, With A Specific 4 Week-Plan, To Lose Weight In A Natural Way And Regain Your Healthy Life

Jennifer J. Hood

Table of Contents

Introduction

The keto diet has received great appreciation and praise for its weight loss benefits. This high-fat, low-carbohydrate diet has been shown to be extremely healthy overall. It really makes your body burn fat, like a talking machine. Public figures also appreciate it. But the question is how does ketosis improve weight loss? Here is a detailed picture of the ketosis and weight loss process.

Ketosis is considered abnormal by some people. Although it has been approved by many nutritionists and doctors. many people still disapprove of it. The misconceptions are due to the myths that have spread around the ketogenic diet.

Once your body has no glucose, it will automatically depend on the stored fat. It is also important to understand that carbohydrates produce glucose, and once you start a low carb diet, you will also be able to lower your glucose levels. Then your body is going to create fuel through fats, instead of carbohydrates, that is, glucose.

The process of creating fat through fat is known as ketosis, and once your body enters this state, it becomes extremely effective in burning unwanted fat. Also, since glucose levels are low during the keto diet, your body achieves many other health benefits.

A ketogenic diet is not only beneficial for weight loss, it also helps improve your overall health in a positive way. Unlike all other diet plans, which focus on reducing calorie intake, keto emphasizes putting your body in a natural metabolic state, namely ketosis. The only factor that makes this diet plan questionable is that this nature of metabolism is not much deliberated. With your body making ketones regularly, your body will quickly burn stored fat, leading to great weight loss.

Now the question arises. How does ketosis affect the human body?

The truth is, a keto diet is healthy for almost everyone. However, we must accept that this diet plan is completely different from what we usually try. Then your body will definitely react a little to the new process. The side effects are called "keto-flu" during which one may experience extreme hunger, low energy levels, lack of sleep and a little nausea.

However, this phase does not last more than 2-3 days. This is the time it takes for the human body to enter the ketosis phase. Once you enter it, you will not have any adverse side effects.

Also, you should gradually start reducing your calorie and carbohydrate intake. The most common mistake dietitians make is that they tend to start eliminating everything from their diet at the same time. This is where the problem arises. The human body will react extremely negatively when you limit everything at once. You need to start gradually. Read this guide for more information on how to approach the keto diet after 50.

Most fats are good and are essential to our healththat's why there are essential fatty acids and essential amino acids (protein). Fats are the most efficient form of energy and each gram contains about 9 calories. That's more than double the amount in carbohydrates and protein (both have 4 calories per gram).

When you eat lots of fat and protein and greatly reduce carbs, your body adapts and converts the fat and protein, as well as the fat you have stored, into ketone bodies, or ketones, for energy. This metabolic process is called ketosis. That's where the ketogenic in ketogenic diet originates from.

This book will provide you with what you need to succeed with the ketogenic diet—simple cooking, weight loss, and long-term success.

CHAPTER 1:

Benefits of Keto for Seniors After 50

There are a lot of benefits in starting a ketogenic diet, be it in terms of weight, experience or to improve your health!

Effective in fighting Epilepsy

The primary goal of this diet, introduced in Antiquity, was to fight against epilepsy. The ketones may affect anti-convulsion, but to date it is not possible to say why they have this effect on the body.

Without going too far into the scientific part, ketone bodies would have an impact on the concentrations of glutamate and GABA (Gamma-Amino Butyric Acid). Glutamate is the main excitatory neuromediator of the central nervous system and GABA the main inhibitory neuromediator. This would explain why the ketogenic diet has such important effects on people with epilepsy. But I don't want to lose you with my scientific explanations, you can do your own research if the subject interests you.

Effective in Weight Loss

Your body's source of energy in the ketogenic diet is fat, either from food or stored by your body. This therefore has advantages: the level of insulin, a hormone that stores fat, drops very significantly, this means that your body will become more efficient at burning fat.

Effective in Type I or Type II Diabetes

The diabetes results in a problem in the metabolism of carbohydrates, the diet is therefore naturally a place to relieve the signs and symptoms in a person with diabetes, whether for a type I or type II diabetes. In fact, whether the problem is a defect in insulin production or insulin resistance, the ketogenic diet will make it possible to get around the problem.

When you are keto-adapted, your blood sugar drops sharply because you only eat foods low in carbohydrates. The ketogenic diet can therefore allow you to control your blood sugar, which can be very effective in managing your diabetes. The ketogenic diet will allow you to reduce your insulin levels to healthy and stable values.

Effective in People with Alzheimer's

Excuse me in advance, but in this part, we will tackle a scientific "hair" side to explain the benefits of the ketogenic diet in the treatment of Alzheimer's disease.

The ketogenic diet is effective in the treatment of neurodegenerative diseases like Alzheimer because it aims to increase the enzymes of the mitochondrial metabolism. Clearly, this would develop more energy in the brain, and therefore improve cognitive efficiency.

In addition to all this, the ketogenic diet would have a role in protecting against oxidative stress, and therefore would be preventive and effective against cell death. This would therefore limit brain degeneration.

Improves Concentration

The ketones are a very good source of fuel for the brain. As you decrease your carbohydrate intake, you avoid blood sugar spikes, which often appear after meals. This allows your body to avoid focusing on eliminating carbohydrates and to focus on the activity you are doing.

Good for Cholesterol

As said above, if you pay attention to the quality of the fats you consume, you will see an improvement in cholesterol: you will see your good cholesterol (HDL: High Density Lipoprotein) increase, while your bad cholesterol (LDL: Low Density Lipoprotein) will decrease.

You will also notice an improvement in triglyceride levels, as well as an improvement in blood pressure. Blood pressure problems are usually caused by being overweight, and the ketogenic diet is intended to cause weight loss and therefore reduce blood pressure problems.

Foods Allowed in Keto Diet

To make the most of your diet, there are prohibited foods, and others that are allowed, but in limited quantities. Here are the foods allowed in the ketogenic diet:

Food allowed in unlimited quantities

Lean or fatty meats

No matter which meat you choose, it contains no carbohydrates so that you can have fun! Pay attention to the quality of your meat, and the amount of fat. Alternate between fatty meats and lean meats!

Here are some examples of lean meats:

Beef: sirloin steak, roast beef, 5% minced steak, roast, flank steak, tenderloin, grisons meat, tripe, kidneys

Horse: roti, steak

Pork: tenderloin, bacon, kidneys

Veal: cutlet, shank, tenderloin, sweetbread, liver

Chicken and turkey: cutlet, skinless thigh, ham

Rabbit

Here are some examples of fatty meats:

Lamb: leg, ribs, brain

Beef: minced steak 10, 15, 20%, ribs, rib steak, tongue, marrow

Pork: ribs, brain, dry ham, black pudding, white pudding, bacon, terrine, rillettes, salami, sausage, sausages, and merguez

Veal: roast, paupiette, marrow, brain, tongue, dumplings

Chicken and turkey: thigh with skin

Guinea fowl

Capon

Turkey

Goose: foie gras

Lean or fatty fish

The fish does not contain carbohydrates so that you can consume unlimited! As with meat, there are lean fish and fatty fish, pay attention to the amount of fat you eat and remember to vary your intake of fish. Oily fish have the advantage of containing a lot of good cholesterol, so it is beneficial for protection against cardiovascular disease! It will be advisable to consume fatty fish more than lean fish, to be able to manage your protein intake: if you consume lean fish, you will have a significant protein intake and little lipids, whereas with fatty fish, you will have a balanced protein and fat intake!

Here are some examples of lean fish:

- Cod

- Colin

- Sea bream

- Whiting

- Sole

- Turbot

- Limor career

- Location

- Pike

- Ray

Here are some examples of oily fish:

- Swordfish

- Salmon

- Tuna

- Trout

- Monkfish

- Herring

- Mackerel

- Cod

- Sardine

Eggs

The eggs contain no carbohydrates, so you can consume as much as you want. It is often said that eggs are full of cholesterol and that you have to limit their intake, but the more cholesterol you eat, the less your body will produce by itself! In addition, it's not just poor-quality cholesterol so that you can consume 6 per week without risk! And if you want to eat more but you are afraid for your cholesterol and I have not convinced you, remove the yellow!

Vegetables and raw vegetables

Yes, you can eat vegetables. But you have to be careful which ones: you can eat leafy vegetables (salad, spinach, kale, red cabbage, Chinese cabbage…) and flower vegetables (cauliflower, broccoli, Romanesco cabbage…) as well as avocado, cucumbers, zucchini or leeks, which do not contain many carbohydrates.

The oils

It's oil, so it's only fat, so it's unlimited to eat, but choose your oil wisely! Prefer olive oil, rapeseed, nuts, sunflower or sesame for example!

Foods authorized in moderate quantities.

The cold cuts

As you know, there is bad cholesterol in cold meats, so you will need to moderate your intake: eat it occasionally!

Fresh cheeses and plain yogurts

Consume with moderation because they contain carbohydrates.

Nuts and oilseeds

They have low levels of carbohydrates, but are rich in saturated fatty acids, that's why they should moderate their consumption. Choose almonds, hazelnuts, Brazil nuts or pecans.

Coconut (in oil, cream or milk)

It contains saturated fatty acids, that's why we limit its consumption. Cream and coconut oil contain a lot of medium chain triglycerides (MCTs), which increase the level of ketones, essential to stay in ketosis.

Berries and red fruits

They contain carbohydrates, in reasonable quantities, but you should not abuse them to avoid ketosis (blueberries, blackberries, raspberries...).

CHAPTER 2:

The Basics of the Keto Diet

What Is A Keto Diet?

The keto diet is a very healthy and natural way to lose weight, but as with most new health regimens, there can be a rather lengthy period of change for some people—for some bodies, I should say. Truly, few will experience what we call the Keto Flu during the beginning of the diet, and it typically lasts about a week, so don't be too concerned if you relate to these symptoms.

You all know that our body needs energy for its functioning and the energy sources come from carbohydrates, proteins, and fats. Owing to years of conditioning that a low-fat carbohydrate-rich diet is essential for good health, we have become used to depending on glucose (from carbohydrates) to get most of the energy that our body needs. Only when the amount of glucose available for energy generation decreases, does our body begin to break down fat for drawing energy to power our cells and organs. This is the express purpose of a ketogenic diet.

The primary aim of a ketogenic diet (called simply as keto diet) is to convert your body into a fat-burning machine. Such a diet is loaded with benefits and is highly recommended by nutritional experts for the following end results:

- Natural appetite control

- Increased mental clarity

- Lowered levels of inflammation in the body system

- Improved stability in blood sugar levels

- Elimination or lower risk of heartburn

- Using natural stored body fat as the fuel source

- Weight loss

The effects listed are just some of the numerous effects that take place when a person embarks on a ketogenic diet and makes it a point to stick to it. A ketogenic diet consists of meals with low carbohydrates, moderate proteins, and high-fat content. The mechanism works like this: when we drastically reduce the intake of carbohydrates, our body is compelled to convert fat for releasing energy. This process of converting fats instead of carbohydrates to release energy is called ketosis.

How Does the Ketogenic Diet Work?

The time has come for you to get the answer to the question that has been lingering in your mind from the time you heard about the keto diet; 'how does a keto diet work?'

Here is how.

The power behind the Ketogenic diet's ability to help you lose weight and have better health comes from one simple action that the diet initiates in your body once you start following it. This simple action is how the keto diet changes your metabolism from burning carbohydrates for energy to burning fats for energy.

What does that have to do with weight loss and better health?

Let me break it down for you.

- Burning carbohydrate for energy

Most of the food we eat follow the food pyramid recommended by the USDA some few decades ago. The pyramid puts carbohydrates at the bottom of the pyramid and fats at the top of the pyramid, which essentially means that carbohydrates form the bulk of the foods we eat, as shown below:

What many of us don't know is that when you consume a diet that is high in carbohydrate, two things normally happen.

- One, your body takes the just consumed carbohydrates and converts it into glucose which is the easiest molecule that your body can convert to use as energy (glucose is your body's primary source of energy, as it gets chosen over any other energy source in your body).

- Secondly, your body produces insulin for the sole purpose of it moving the glucose from your bloodstream into your cells where it can be used as energy.

There is more that goes unnoticed though:

Since your body gets its energy from glucose (which is mostly in huge amounts owing to the fact that we eat lots of high carb food 3-6 times a day), it doesn't need any other source of energy. In fact, many are the times when glucose is in excess, something that prompts the body to convert dietary glucose into glycogen to be stored in the liver and muscle cells. What this simple explanation means is that with a high carb diet, your body is essentially in what we refer to as a fat-storing mode. It stores this excess fat so that it can use it when starved from its primary source of energy; glucose. Unfortunately, since we don't give ourselves enough breaks from food, we end up being in this constant fat-storing mode that ultimately causes weight gain.

- Burning fats for energy

As you now know, the Ketogenic diet is a low carb, high fat, and moderate protein diet. So, when you start following a Ketogenic diet, what typically happens is, your intake of carbohydrate is kept at a low. In other words, it inverts the USDA food pyramid I mentioned earlier, something that literally 'inverts/reverses' the effects of a high carb diet.

How exactly does it do that?

Well, when you limit your carb intake greatly, you starve the body of its primary source of energy, something that initiates the process that the body has always been preparing for through its energy storage processes. More specifically, the body starts by metabolizing glycogen with the help of glucagon hormone (the process takes place in the liver). And with support from the human growth hormone, cortisol, and catecholamines (norepinephrine to be more specific), the body starts releasing fatty acids for use as energy in different body parts. But since fatty acids cannot be used by every cell in the body, the body is also forced to transport some of the fatty acids to the liver where they are broken down in a series of metabolic processes known as ketosis to produce 3 ketone bodies. Therefore, Ketosis is a natural process that your body activates when your energy intake is low for the purpose of helping you to survive. The three ketones that are formed when fatty acids are converted are:

- Acetone.

- Beta-hydroxybutyric acid (BHB)

- Acetoacetate (AcAc)

Many of your body cells (including the brain cells) can use BHB for energy, as it is water-soluble, something that makes it very much like glucose in that it can cross the-blood brain barrier. The more ketones the body cells use for energy, the more fat you are burning and ultimately, the more weight you stand to gain. Keep in mind that you are also taking lots of dietary fats. The reason for taking lots of dietary fats is to fill you up fast, make you to stay full for longer and accustom the body cells to using fatty acids and ketones for energy so that when the deficit created by dietary fats kicks in (because you are unlikely to eat so much fats to the point of meeting your body's energy requirements- unless you are gluttonous), you begin burning stored body fat immediately, as opposed to starting with glycogen. Moderate intake of protein also helps you to get filled fast and to stay full for longer. Keeping your protein intake moderate is therefore vital, as any excess may end up causing you to get out of ketosis, as excess protein may be metabolized to glucose in a process known as gluconeogenesis. This essentially means a Ketogenic diet makes your body a fat-burning machine, as it relies primarily on fats (both dietary and stored body fat – though you want to get your body to burn as much of the stored boy fat as possible).

Ketosis helps you get rid of excessive fats in your body, which not only reduce your weight in an immense way but also betters your health by protecting you from various diseases as you will see.

To attain ketosis, you know that your intake of fats should be high, intake of carbs low and intake of proteins moderate. But what exactly does high, low and moderate translate to in calorie terms? In simpler terms, in what ratios should you take carbs, fats, and proteins? This gives rise to several types/approaches/schools of thought regarding the ratios:

Who invented this diet?

The ketogenic diet traces its roots to the treatment of epilepsy. Surprisingly this goes all the way back to 500 BC, when ancient Greeks observed that fasting or eating a ketogenic diet helped reduce epileptic seizures. In modern times, the ketogenic diet was reintroduced in the practice of medicine to treat children with epilepsy.

What is Ketosis?

Ketosis is a metabolic state where the body is efficiently using fat for energy. In a regular diet, carbohydrates produce glucose, which is used to provide energy. Glucose is stored in the body in fat cells that travel via the bloodstream. People gain weight when there is fatter stored than being used as energy.

Glucose is formed through the consumption of sugar and starch. Namely carbohydrates. The sugars may be in the form of natural sugars from fruit or milk, or they may be formed from processed sugar. Starches like pasta, rice or starchy vegetables like potatoes and corn, form glucose as well. The body breaks down the sugars from these foods into glucose. Glucose and insulin combined to help to carry glucose into the bloodstream so the body can use glucose as energy. The glucose that is not used is stored in the liver and muscles.

In order for the body to supply ketones for use as fuel, the body must use up all the reserves of glucose. In order to do this, there must be a condition of the body of starvation low carbohydrates, passing, or strenuous exercise. A very low carb diet, the production of ketones what her to feel the body and brain.

Ketones are produced from the liver when there is not enough glucose in the body to provide energy. When insulin levels are low, and there is not enough glucose or sugar in the bloodstream, fat is released from fat cells and travels in the blood to the liver. The liver processes the fat into ketones. Ketones are released into the bloodstream to provide fuel for the body and increase the body's metabolism. Ketones are formed under conditions of starvation, fasting, or a diet low in carbohydrates.

CHAPTER 3:

How Keto Diet Affects 50 Old Women

Women who are looking for a quick and effective way to shed excess weight, get high blood sugar levels under control, reduce overall inflammations, and improve physical and mental energy will do their best by following a ketogenic diet plan. But there are special considerations women must take into account when they are beginning the keto diet.

All women know it is much more difficult for women to lose weight than it is for men to lose weight. A woman will live on a starvation level diet and exercise like a triathlete and only lose five pounds. A man will stop putting dressing on his salad and will lose twenty pounds. It just is not fair. But we have the fact that we are women to blame. Women naturally have more standing between them and weight loss than men do.

The mere fact that we are women is the largest single contributor to the reason we find it difficult to lose weight. Since our bodies always think they need to be prepared for the possibility of pregnancy women will naturally have more body fat and less mass in our muscles than men will. Muscle cells burn more calories than fat cells do. So, because we are women, we will always lose weight more slowly than men will.

Being in menopause will also cause women to add more pounds to their bodies, especially in the lower half of the body. After menopause a woman's metabolism naturally slows down. Your hormones levels will decrease. These two factors alone will cause weight gain in the post-menopausal woman.

Women are a direct product of their hormones. Men also have hormones but not the ones like we have that regulate every function in our bodies. And the hormones in women will fluctuate around their everyday habits like lack of sleep, poor eating habits, and menstrual cycles. These hormones cause women to crave sweets around the time their periods occur. These cravings will wreck any diet plan. Staying true to the keto plan is challenging at this time because of the intense craving for sweets and carbs. Also having your period will often make you feel and look bloated because of the water your body holds onto during this time. And having cramps make you more likely to reach for a bag of cookies than a plate of steak and salad.

Because we are women, we may experience challenges on the keto diet that men will not face because they are men. One of these challenges is having weight loss plateau or even experiencing weight gain. This can happen because of the influence of hormones on weight loss in women. If this happens you will want to increase your consumption of good fats like ghee, butter, eggs, coconut oil, beef, avocados, and olive oil. Any food that is cooked or prepared using oil must be prepared in olive oil or avocado oil.

You can also use MCT oil. MCT stands for medium chain triglycerides. This is a form of fatty acid that is saturated and has many health benefits. MCT can help with many body functions from weight loss to improved brain function. MCTs are mostly missing from the typical American diet because we have been told that saturated fats are harmful to the body, and as a group they are. But certain saturated fats, like MCTs, are actually beneficial to the body, especially when they come from good foods like beef or coconut oil. They are easier to digest than most other saturated fats and may help improve heart and brain function and prevent obesity.

Many women on a keto diet will struggle with imbalances in their hormones. On the keto diet you do not rely on lowered calories to lose weight but on foods effect on your hormones. So, when women begin the keto diet any issues, they are already having with their hormones will be brought to attention and may cause the woman to give up before she really begins. Always remember that the keto diet is responsible for cleansing the system first so that the body can easily respond to the wonderful affects a keto diet has to offer.

Do not try to work toward the lean body that many men sport. It is best for overall function that women stay at twenty-two to twenty six percent body fat. Our hormones will function best in this range and we can't possibly function without our hormones. Women who are very lean, like gymnasts and extreme athletes, will find their hormones no longer function or function at a less than optimal rate. And remember that ideal weight may not be the right weight for you. Many women find that they perform their best when they are at their happy weight. If you find yourself fighting with yourself to lose the last few pounds you think you need to lose in order to have the perfect body then it may not be worth it. The struggle will affect your hormone function. Carefully observing the keto diet will allow time for your hormones to stabilize and regulate themselves back to their pre-obesity normal function.

Like any other diet plan the keto diet will work better if you are active. Regular exercise will allow the body to strengthen and tone muscles and will help to work off excess fat reserves. But exercise requires energy to accomplish. If you restrict your carb intake too much you might not have the energy needed to be physically able to make it all the way through the day and still be able to maintain an exercise routine. You might need to add in more carbs to your diet through the practice of carb cycling.

As a woman you know that sometimes your emotions get the better of you. This is true with your body, as you well know, and can be a major reason why women find it extremely difficult at times to lose weight the way they want to lose weight. We have been led to believe that not only can we do it all but that we must do it all. This gives many women unnecessary levels of pressure and can cause them to engage in emotional eating. Some women might have lowered feelings of self-worth and may not feel they are entitled to the benefits of the keto diet, and turning to food relieves the feelings of inadequacy that we try to hide from the world.

When you engage in the same activity for a long period of time it becomes a habit. When you reach for the bag of potato chips or the tub of ice cream whenever you are angry, upset, or depressed, then your brain will eventually tell you to reach for food whenever you feel an emotion that you don't want to deal with. Food acts as a security blanket against the world outside. It may be necessary to address any extreme emotional issues you are having before you begin the keto diet, so that you are better assured of success.

The basic act of staying on the keto diet can be very challenging for some women. Many women see beginning a new diet to lose weight as a punishment for being overweight. It may be worthwhile for you to work at changing the set of your mind if you are feeling this way. You may need to remind yourself daily that the keto diet is not a punishment but a blessing for your body. Tell yourself that you are not denying yourself certain foods because you can't eat them, but because you do not like the way those foods make your body feel. Don't watch other people eating their high carb diet and pity yourself. Instead, feel sorry for the people who have trapped themselves in a high calorie diet and are not experiencing the benefits that you are experiencing.

And for the first thirty days cut out all sweeteners, even the non-sugar ones that are allowed on the keto diet. While they may make food taste better, they also remind your brain that it needs sweet foods when it really doesn't. Cutting them out for at least thirty days will break the cycle that your body has fallen into and will cut the cravings for sweets in your diet.

It is very possible for women to be successful on the keto diet if they are prepared to follow a few simple adjustments that will make the diet look differently than your male partner might be eating but that will make you successful in the long run.

During the first one or two weeks you will need to consume extra fat than a man might need to. Doing this will have three important effects on your body. First it will cause your mitochondria to intensify their acceptance of your new way of finding energy. Mitochondria are tiny organisms that are found in cells and are responsible for using the fuel that insulin brings to the cell for fuel for the cell. Increasing your fat intake will also help make sure you are getting enough calories in your daily diet. This is important because if your body thinks you are starving it will begin to conserve calories and you will stop losing weight.

The third benefit from eating more fat, and perhaps the most important, is the psychological boost you will get from seeing that you can eat more fat and still lose weight and feel good. It will also reset your mindset that you formerly might have held against fat. For so long we have been told that low fat is the only way to lose weight. But an absence of dietary fat will lead to overeating and binge eating out of a feeling of deprivation. When you begin the diet by allowing yourself to eat a lot, or too much in your mind, fat, then you swing the pendulum around to the other side of the fat scale where it properly belongs. You teach yourself that fat can be good for you. Increasing the extra intake of fats should not last beyond the second week of the diet. Your body will improve its abilities to create and burn ketones and body fat, and then you will begin using your own body fat for fuel and you can begin to lower your reliance on dietary fat a little bit so that you will begin to lose weight.

The keto diet is naturally lower in calories if you follow the recommended levels of food intake. It is not necessary to try to restrict your intake of calories even further. All you need to do is to eat only until you are full and not one bite more. Besides losing weight the aim of the keto diet is to retrain your body on how to work properly. You will need to learn to trust your body and the signals it sends out to be able to readjust to a proper way of eating.

CHAPTER 4:

Types of keto Diet

There are several types of Ketogenic diet that you could adapt and maintain. These include;

The Standard Ketogenic Diet (SKD): In simple terms, this is a very low-carb diet accompanied by high-fats and average protein that is consumed by human beings. It consists of 70% to 75% fats, 20% protein and about 5% to 10% carbs. This translates to about 20 – 45 grams of carbohydrates, 40 – 65 grams of proteins, but no set limits for fats, which makes up for large parts of the diet. This is because fats are what provides the calories which constitute energy and make the diet a successful Ketogenic diet. Additionally, there is no limit to the fats because different human beings have different energy requirements. The Standard Ketogenic Diet is successful in assisting people in losing weight, improving the body's glucose as well as improving heart health.

Targeted Ketogenic Diet (TKD): This type of Ketogenic Diet focuses its attention on the addition of carbs during workout sessions only. This type of Ketogenic diet is almost similar to the Standard Ketogenic Diet except for the fact that carbohydrates are all but consumed during workout sessions. This type of diet is solely based on the idea that the body will effectively and efficiently process carbohydrates consumed before or during a workout session. This is because the diet assumes that the muscles would be bound to demand more energy, which would be provided by the carbohydrates consumed and be processed quickly since the body is in an active state. This diet, in simpler terms, is a diet caught up between the Cyclical Ketogenic diet and the Standard Ketogenic Diet, which allows room for consumption of carbohydrates on the days that you would decide to work out only.

High-Protein Ketogenic Diet: This type of Ketogenic Diet advocates for more protein compared to the Standard Ketogenic Diet. This diet consists of 35% protein, 60% fats, and 5% carbs, unlike the Standard Ketogenic Diet. Research has greatly suggested that this diet would be effective for you if you are attempting to lose weight. However, unlike other types of the Ketogenic diet, no research has been dedicated to showing if there are any side effects of adapting to the diet for elongated periods of time.

Recurring Ketogenic Diet (RKD): This kind of Ketogenic Diet focuses on higher-carb re-feeds, for instance, 5 Ketogenic days and 2 high-carb days, and this cycle is repeated. This diet is also known as the carb backloading and is often intended for athletes because the diet allows their bodies to recover the glycogen lost as a result of workouts or intense sporting activities.

Very low carbs Ketogenic diet (VLCKD): As stated prior, a Ketogenic diet will most likely consist of very low carbs; thus, this diet often refers to the characteristics of the Standard Ketogenic Diet.

The Well Formulated Ketogenic Diet: this term is as a result of one of the leading researchers into the Ketogenic diet, Steve Phinney. As the name suggests, this diet has its fats, carbohydrates, and proteins well formulated and that it meets the standards of a Ketogenic diet. This diet is also similar to the Standard Ketogenic Diet, and this means that it creates room for your body to undergo ketosis effectively.

The MCT Ketogenic Diet: The diet is also related to the Standard Ketogenic Diet only that it derives most of its fats from medium-chain triglycerides (MCTs). This diet will often use coconut oil, which has high levels of MCTs. This diet has been reported to efficiently treat epilepsy because of its concept that MCTs give your body enough room to consume carbohydrates as well as proteins and still maintain your body's ketosis. This is a result of MCTs providing more ketones per gram in fat, contrary to the long-chain triglycerides, which are more common in the normal dietary fats. However, MCTs could lead to diarrhea as well as stomach upsets if this diet is consumed in large quantities on its own. To handle, it is wise to prepare a meal with a balance of both MCTs and fats with no MCTs. There is no evidence to prove that this diet could as well have benefits in your attempt to losing weight or if the diet could regulate your body's blood sugar.

The Calorie Restricted Ketogenic Diet: This is also related to the Standard Ketogenic Diet except that its calories are only limited to a given amount only. Research has proven that Ketogenic diets could be successful whether the consumption of calories is restricted or not. The reason behind this is that the effect of consuming fats and your body being in ketosis is a way in itself that prevents you from over-eating or eating beyond your limits.

There are numerous Ketogenic diets, but the Standard Ketogenic Diet and the High-Protein Ketogenic Diets are the most studied and most recommended for health issues. The Repeated (cyclical) and Targeted Ketogenic diets remain mostly practiced by athletes and bodybuilders and are more advanced than the Standard Ketogenic Diet and the High-Protein Ketogenic Diet. Visit and consult your local physician before opting to settle on any of the types of Ketogenic diets.

CHAPTER 5:

Most Common Mistakes and How to Fix Them

Do you feel like you are giving your all to the keto diet but you still aren't seeing the results you want? You are measuring ketones, working out, and counting your macros, but you still aren't losing the weight you want. Here are the most common mistakes that most people make when beginning the keto diet.

1. Too Many Snacks

There are many snacks you can enjoy while following the keto diet, like nuts, avocado, seeds, and cheese. But snacking can be an easy way to get too many calories into the diet while giving your body an easy fuel source besides stored fat. Snacks need to be only used if you frequently hunger between meals. If you aren't extremely hungry, let your body turn to your stored fat for its fuel between meals instead of dietary fat.

2. Not Consuming Enough Fat

The ketogenic diet isn't all about low carbs. It's also about high fats. You need to be getting about 75 percent of your calories from healthy fats, five percent from carbs, and 20 percent from protein. Fat makes you feel fuller longer, so if you eat the correct amount, you will minimize your carb cravings, and this will help you stay in ketosis. This will help your body burn fat faster.

3. Consuming Excessive Calories

You may hear people say you can eat what you want on the keto diet as long as it is high in fat. Even though we want that to be true, it is very misleading. Healthy fats need to make up the biggest part of your diet. If you eat more calories than what you are burning, you will gain weight, no matter what you eat because these excess calories get stored as fat. An average adult only needs about 2,000 calories each day, but this will vary based on many factors like activity level, height, and gender.

4. Consuming a lot of Dairies

For many people, dairy can cause inflammation and keeps them from losing weight. Dairy is a combo food meaning it has carbs, protein, and fats. If you eat a lot of cheese as a snack for the fat content, you are also getting a dose of carbs and protein with that fat. Many people can tolerate dairy, but moderation is the key. Stick with no more than one to two ounces of cheese or cream at each meal. Remember to factor in the protein content.

5. Consuming a lot of Protein

The biggest mistake that most people make when just beginning the keto diet is consuming too much protein. Excess protein gets converted into glucose in the body called gluconeogenesis. This is a natural process where the body converts the energy from fats and proteins into glucose when glucose isn't available. When following a ketogenic diet, gluconeogenesis happens at different rates to keep body function. Our bodies don't need a lot of carbs, but we do need glucose. You can eat absolute zero carbs, and through gluconeogenesis, your body will convert other substances into glucose to be used as fuel. This is why carbs only make up five percent of your macros. Some parts of our bodies need carbs to survive, like kidney, medulla, and red blood cells. With gluconeogenesis, our bodies make and stores extra glucose as glycogen just in case supplies become too low.

In a normal diet, when carbs are always available, gluconeogenesis happens slowly because the need for glucose is extremely low. Our body runs on glucose and will store excess protein and carbs as fat.

It does take time for our bodies to switch from using glucose to burning fats. Once you are in ketosis, your body will use fat as the main fuel source and will start to store excess protein as glycogen.

6. Not Getting Enough Water

Water is crucial for your body. Water is needed for all your body does, and this includes burning fat. If you don't drink enough water, it can cause your metabolism to slow down, and this can halt your weight loss. Drinking 64 ounces or one-half gallon every day will help your body burn fat, flush out toxins, and circulate nutrients. When you are just beginning the keto diet, you might need to drink more water since your body will begin to get rid of body fat by flushing it out through urine.

7. Consuming Too Many Sweets

Some people might indulge in keto brownies and keto cookies that are full of sugar substitute just because their net carb content is low, but you have to remember that you are still eating calories. Eating sweets might increase your carb cravings. Keto sweets are great on occasion; they don't need to be a staple in the diet.

8. Not Getting Enough Sleep

Getting plenty of sleep is needed in order to lose weight effectively. Without the right amount of sleep, your body will feel stressed, and this could result in your metabolism slowing down. It might cause it to store fat instead of burning fat. When you feel tired, you are more tempted to drink more lattes for energy, eat a snack to give you an extra boost, or order takeout rather than cooking a healthy meal. Try to get between seven and nine hours of sleep each night. Understand that your body uses that time to burn fat without you even lifting a finger.

9. Low on Electrolytes

Most people will experience the keto flu when you begin this diet. This happens for two reasons when your body changes from burning carbs to burning fat, your brain might not have enough energy, and this, in turn, can cause grogginess, headaches, and nausea. You could be dehydrated, and your electrolytes might be low since the keto diet causes you to urinate often.

Getting the keto flu is a great sign that you are heading in the right direction. You can lessen these symptoms by drinking more water or taking supplements that will balance your electrolytes.

10. Consuming Hidden Carbs

Many foods look like they are low carb, but they aren't. You can find carbs in salad dressings, sauces, and condiments. Be sure to check nutrition labels before you try new foods to make sure it doesn't have any hidden sugar or carbs. It just takes a few seconds to skim the label, and it might be the difference between whether or not you'll lose weight.

If you have successfully ruled out all of the above, but you still aren't losing weight, you might need to talk with your doctor to make sure you don't have any health problems that could be preventing your weight loss. This can be frustrating, but stick with it, stay positive, and stay in the game. When the keto diet is done correctly, it is one of the best ways to lose weight.

CHAPTER 6:

Tips for Success

Routines are very important on this diet, and it's something that will help you stay healthy. As such, in this chapter, we are going to be giving you tips and tricks to make this diet work better for you and help you get an idea of routines that you can put in place for yourself.

Tip number one that is so important is DRINK WATER! This is absolutely vital for any diet that you're on, and you need it if not on one as well. However, this vital tip is crucial on a keto diet because when you are eating fewer carbs, you are storing less water, meaning that you are going to get dehydrated very easily. You should aim for more than the daily amount of water however, remember that drinking too much water can be fatal as your kidneys can only handle so much as once. While this has mostly happened to soldiers in the military, it does happen to dieters as well, so it is something to be aware of.

Along with that same tip is to keep your electrolytes. You have three major electrolytes in your body. When you are on a keto diet, your body is reducing the amount of water that you store. It can be flushing out the electrolytes that your body needs as well, and this can make you sick. Some of the ways that you can fight this is by either salting your food or drinking bone broth. You can also eat pickled vegetables.

Eat when you're hungry instead of snacking or eating constantly. This is also going to help, and when you focus on natural foods and health foods, this will help you even more. Eating processed foods is the worst thing you can do for fighting cravings, so you should really get into the routine of trying to eat whole foods instead.

Another routine that you can get into is setting a note somewhere that you can see it that will remind you of why you're doing this in the first place and why it's important to you. Dieting is hard, and you will have moments of weakness where you're wondering why you are doing this. Having a reminder will help you feel better, and it can really help with your perspective.

Tracking progress is something that straddles the fence. A Lot of people say that this helps a lot of people and you can celebrate your wins, however, as everyone is different and they have different goals, progress can be slower in some than others. This can cause others to be frustrated and sad, as well as wanting to give up. One of the most important things to remember is that while progress takes time, and you shouldn't get discouraged if you don't see results right away. With most diets, it takes at least a month to see any results. So, don't get discouraged and keep trying if your body is saying that you can. If you can't, then you will need to talk to your doctor and see if something else is for you.

You should make it a daily routine to try and lower your stress. Stress will not allow you to get into ketosis, which is that state that keto wants to put you in. The reason for this being that stress increases the hormone known as cortisol in your blood, and it will prevent your body from being able to burn fats for energy. This is because your body has too much sugar in your blood. If you're going through a really high period of stress right now in your life, then this diet is not a great idea. Some great ideas for this would be getting into the habit or routine of taking the time to do something relaxing, such as walking and making sure that you're getting enough sleep, leads to the following routine that you need to do.

You need to get enough sleep. This is so important not just for your diet but also for your mind and body as well. Poor sleep also raises those stress hormones that can cause issues for you, so you need to get into the routine of getting seven hours of sleep at night on the minimum and nine hours if you can. If you're getting less than this, you need to change the routine you have in place right now and make sure that you establish a new routine where you are getting more sleep. As a result, your health and diet will be better.

Another routine that you need to get into is to give up diet soda and sugar substitutes. This is going to help you with your diet as well because diet soda can actually increase your sugar levels to a bad amount, and most diet sodas contain aspartame. This can be a carcinogen, so it's actually quite dangerous. Another downside is that using these sugar substitutes just makes you want more sugar. Instead, you need to get into the habit of drinking water or sparkling water if you like the carbonation.

Staying consistent is another routine that you need to get yourself into. No matter what you are choosing to do, make sure it's something that you can actually do. Try a routine for a couple of weeks and make serious notes of mental and physical problems that you're going through as well as any emotional issues that come your way. Make changes as necessary until you find something that works well for you and that you can stick to. Remember that you need to give yourself time to get used to this and time to get used to changes before you give up on them.

Be honest with yourself, as well. This is another big tip for this diet. If you're not honest with yourself, this isn't going to work. Another reason that you need to be honest with yourself is if something isn't working you need to be able to understand that and change it. Are you giving yourself enough time to make changes? Are you pushing too hard? If so, you need to understand what is going on with yourself and how you need to deal with the changes that you're going through. Remember not to get upset or frustrated. This diet takes time, and you need to be able to be a little more patient to make this work effectively.

Getting into the routine of cooking for yourself is also going to help you so much on this diet. Eating out is fun, but honestly, on this diet, it can be hard to eat out. It is possible to do so with a little bit of special ordering and creativity, but you can avoid all the trouble by simply cooking for yourself. It saves time, and it saves a lot of cash.

This subsequent topic falls into both the tip and routine category. Get into the habit of cleaning your kitchen. It's very hard to stick to a diet if your kitchen is dirty and full of junk food. Clear out the junk (donate it if you can, even though it's junk, there are tons of hungry people that would appreciate it) and replace all of the bad food with healthy keto food instead. Many people grab the carbs like crazy because they haven't cleared out their cabinets, and it's everywhere they look. Remember, with this diet, no soda, pasta, bread, candy, and things of that nature. Replacing your food with healthy food and making a regular routine of cleaning your kitchen and keeping the bad food out is going to help you be more successful with your diet, which is what you want here.

Getting into the routine of having snacks on hand is a good idea as well. This keeps you from giving into temptation while you're out, and you can avoid reaching for that junk food. You can make sure that they are healthy, and you will be sticking to your high-intensity diet, which is what you want. There are many different keto snacks that you can use for yourself and to eat. We will have a list of recipes in the following chapters to help this as well.

A good tip would be to use keto sticks or a glucose meter. This will give you feedback on whether your users do this diet right. The best option here is a glucose meter. It's expensive, but it's the most accurate. Be aware that if you use ketostix, they are cheaper, but the downside is that they are not accurate enough to help you. A perfect example is that they have a habit of telling people their ketone count is low when they are actually the opposite.

Try not to overeat as this will throw you out of where you need to be. Get into the routine of paying attention to what you're eating and how much. If this is something that you're struggling with, try investing in a food scale. You will be able to see exactly what it is your eating and make sure that your understanding your portions and making sure you stay in ketosis.

Another tip is to make sure that you're improving your gut health. This is so important. Your gut is pretty much linked to every other system in your body, so make sure that this something that you want to take seriously. When you have healthy gut flora, your body's hormones, along with your insulin sensitivity and metabolic flexibility will all be more efficient. When your flexibility is functioning at an optimal level, your body is able to adapt to your diet easier. If it's not, then it will convert the fat your trying to use for energy into body fat.

Batch cooking or meal prepping is another routine that is a good thing to get into. This is an especially good routine for on the go women. When you cook in batches, you are able to make sure that you have meals that are ready to go, and you don't have to cook every single day, and you can save a lot of time as well. You will also be making your environment better for your diet because you're supporting your goals instead of working against them.

The last tip is to mention exercise again. Getting into the routine of exercising can boost your ketone levels, and it can help you with your issues on transitioning to keto. Exercises also use different types of energy for your fuel that you need. When your body gets rid of the glycogen storages, it needs other forms of energy, and it will turn into that energy that you need. Just remember to avoid exercises that are going to hurt you. Stay in the smaller exercises and lower intensity.

Following these tips and getting into these routines is going to help you stay on track and make sure that your diet will go as smoothly as it possibly can.

CHAPTER 7:

Entering a State of Ketosis to Lose Weight and Stay Healthy

Ketogenic Vs Low Carb

Keto and low carbohydrate diets are similar in many ways. On a ketogenic diet, the body moves to a ketosis state, and the brain is ultimately powered by ketones. These are produced in the liver when the intake of carbohydrates is very small. Low carbohydrate diets may entail diverse things for different people. Low-carb diets actually reduce your overall carbohydrate consumption.

For regular low-carb diets, brain habits are still mostly glucose-dependent, although they may consume higher ketones than standard diets. To accomplish this, you'd have to follow low-carb, low-calorie, and an active lifestyle. The amount of carbohydrate you eat depends on the type of diet you consume.

At the end of the day, low carb is reduced in your carb intake. Mentions can vary enormously depending on the number of total carbs consumed per day. People have different views and follow different rules, from 0 to 100 grams of net carbs. Though a ketogenic diet has low carbohydrates, it also has significantly low protein levels. The overall increase in blood levels of ketones is significant.

What Is Ketosis?

When you reduce the intake of carbs over a period of time, the body can begin to break down body fat for energy for daily tasks. This is a natural occurrence called ketosis that the body undergoes to help us survive while food intake is small. We create ketones during this process, produced from the breakdown of fats in the liver. Once ketones are processed into energy, they are a byproduct of fatty acids.

Blood ketone bodies also increase substantially to higher than normal levels. Mind, muscle and all tissue that includes mitochondria utilize ketones. With practice, you'll soon learn how to understand ketosis signs.

A properly controlled ketogenic diet has the function of pushing your body into the metabolic state to consume fats as energy. Not by depriving the body of calories but by eliminating sugars. The bodies are outstandingly resilient to what you place in them. Taking keto nutrients such as keto OS can improve cell regeneration, strength, and lifespan. If an excess of fats is available, and carbs are eliminated, ketones can continue to burn as the primary source of energy.

Can A Keto Diet Help You Lose Weight?

There are different ways that a ketogenic diet will help a person shed excess fat in their body to meet their target weight. Scientists are still doing thorough research to understand just how this whole process works and how precisely the condition of ketosis helps an individual in terms of losing their excess weight.

Because protein intake is improved in most situations when a person moves to a ketogenic diet, and there are many healthy eating choices, including some veggies, that are filled with fiber in this specific type of diet, one of the most popular reasons would be better satiety. For texture and protein, you'll find that you don't feel hungry as long as you've had a meal similar to before you had such same meals and you've decided to follow the diet.

With improved satiety and dieting plans, binge eating is something that can usually be avoided effectively. If you don't feel hungry between the main meals of the day, there's little need for a bag of potato chips or an energy bar.

Nonetheless, there would be moments where hunger hits—in such situations, carrying a handful of nuts can be a very healthy alternative to those energy bars, donuts, and other unhealthy, dangerous snacks that you usually choose when you find you need to consume when it's not time for the following meal.

CHAPTER 8:

4 Weeks Meal Plan

Week	Days	Breakfast	Lunch	Dinner
Week 1	1	Egg Muffins or Tortilla Muffins Chickpea Flour or Pure Peanut Butter Meal	Fiesta chicken salad or easy broccoli salad with almond and lemon sauce	Banana slices with peanut butter
	2	Egg or Chickpea Muffins Remaining or Peanut Butter Oatmeal	shrimp with garlic in coconut milk, tomatoes and coriander or zucchini, peas and spinach risotto	apple with a sunflower / pumpkin combination
	3	Clean eating egg and basil vegetable stir or tofu factory	Remaining taco salad or wild rice burrito bowl	Celery with peanut butter and raisins
	4	Berry oatmeal	Tuna salad with avocado or sliced tofu pesto sandwich	Pieces of cucumber with hummus
	5	Muesli	Tuscan Stewed Beans	Green Egg Scramble

	6	Protein pancakes or old vegan pancakes	Orange and almond salad with avocado or fall harvest salad with pomegranate vinaigrette snack: popcorn with egg	Pear and peanuts
	7	Hot protein or vegan pancakes	Zucchini pasta with seafood or zucchini pasta with avocado	baby carrots with guacamole
Week 2	8	Flourless banana and chocolate pumpkin muffins or raspberry and pumpkin muffins	chicken and remaining orange salad or orange tofu	brown rice salad, peanut butter and a tablespoon of honey or maple syrup
	9	Apple and bacon sandwich	Toasted grilled salmon with mango sauce or smoked tempeh	Banana and zucchini muffins without chocolate
	10	Egg muffins or sun-dried tomato cake.	Bowl of mushrooms and cauliflower	Baked sweet potato with peanut butter, banana and cinnamon
	11	Breakfast: apple and bacon sandwich	Waldorf chicken salad with avocado or vegan Waldorf salad	cherry or vegan yolks
	12	Remains of breakfast yolks or vegan yolks	Banana pieces with vanilla butter and cocoa powder.	carrots and hummus

	13	Breakfast: sweet potato toast	salad with avocado and shrimp (using the rest of the beans) or sweet and sour tofu	Bony popcorn with hard-boiled eggs or some grilled chickpeas
	14	Breakfast: sweet potato toast	roasted dry herb and garlic sandwich: Larabar	pieces of cucumber and hummus
Week 3	15	Breakfast: cereals with berries, veal and coconut.	citrus chicken strips on a spinach salad	boiled eggs or two roasted chickpeas and carrots with hummus
	16	Breakfast: cereals with berries, veal and coconut.	citrus chicken strips on a spinach salad	boiled eggs or two roasted chickpeas and carrots with hummus
	17	Breakfast: oatmeal spices	vintage chicken salad or lentil cucumber salad	Brown rice with peanut butter and banana piece.
	18	Breakfast: left-over apple spice overnight oats	left-over harvest chicken salad or lentil cucumber salad	apple and couple roasted chickpeas
	19	Breakfast: fresh fruit and rice	Greek quinoa salad	banana and pistachios
	20	Breakfast: black bean scramble or spiced chickpea	leftovers – green quinoa salad	chocolate cherry energy bites

	21	Breakfast: banana oat protein muffins	left-over homemade chicken noodle soup or curried butternut squash soup	apple chips dipped in peanut butter
Week 4	22	Purple sweet potato salmon sushi roll and coffee with heavy cream.	Keto buffalo chicken meatball	Bacon-armesan Spaghetti Squash and Grilled beef roast.
	23	Eggs of any style and coffee with heavy cream without any carb sweetener.	Keto chocolate Greek yoghurt cookies and Keto beef and sausage balls	Coconut Crab Cakes and Olive-flavored pork broth
	24	Cream Cheese Pancakes, coffee with heavy cream	Leftover 10-minute chili, tuna salad, or ham and cheese/pancake rollups.	Easy Cajun Chicken, Cheesy Cauliflower Puree, and 2 cups baby spinach with carb-free dressing
	25	Fish balls with chives with lemon garlic cream sauce and Bulletproof coffee.	Keto pizza and Tangerine avocado smoothie	Cheesy bacon ranch chicken
	26	Keto pizza bites with keto flaxseeds bread	Keto Tuna melt with a side salad and Keto coconut flavored	Keto catfish soup and Cheesy-chicken roast

			ice cream	
	27	Keto meatballs with full-fat yoghurt.	Chicken Caesar salad	Pot roast beef with buttery asparagus.
	28	Keto scrambled eggs with keto iced tea	Grilled salmon with a side salad.	Ground beef with cheesy cauliflower mash.

CHAPTER 9:

Breakfast Recipes

Overnight "noats"

Preparation Time: 5 minutes plus overnight to chill

Cooking time: 10 minutes

Servings: 1

Ingredients:

2 tablespoons hulled hemp seeds

1 tablespoon chia seeds

½ scoop (about 8 grams) collagen powder

½ cup unsweetened nut or seed milk (hemp, almond, coconut, and cashew)

Direction:

In a small mason jar or glass container, combine the hemp seeds, chia seeds, collagen, and milk.

Secure tightly with a lid, shake well, and refrigerate overnight.

Nutrition:

Calories: 263- Total Fat: 19g - Protein: 16g - Total Carbs: 7g - Fiber: 5g - Net Carbs: 2g

Frozen keto coffee

Preparation Time: 5 minutes

Cooking time: 20 minutes

Servings: 1

Ingredients: 12 ounces coffee, chilled

1 scoop MCT powder (or 1 tablespoon MCT oil)

1 tablespoon heavy (whipping) cream

Pinch ground cinnamon

Dash sweetener (optional)

½ cup ice

Directions:

In a blender, combine the coffee, MCT powder, cream, cinnamon, sweetener (if using), and ice. Blend until smooth.

Nutrition:

Calories: 127; Total Fat: 13g;

Protein: 1g; Total Carbs: 1.5g;

Fiber: 1g; Net Carbs: 0.5g

No-Bake Keto Power Bars

Preparation Time: 10 Minutes

Cooking time: 0 minutes

Servings: 12 bars

Ingredients:

½ cup pili nuts

½ cup whole hazelnuts

½ cup walnut halves

¼ cup hulled sunflower seeds

¼ cup unsweetened coconut flakes or chips

¼ cup hulled hemp seeds

2 tablespoons unsweetened cacao nibs

2 scoops collagen powder (I use 1 scoop Perfect Keto vanilla collagen and 1 scoop Perfect Keto unflavored collagen powder)

½ teaspoon ground cinnamon

½ teaspoon sea salt

¼ cup coconut oil, melted

1 teaspoon vanilla extract

Stevia or monk fruit to sweeten (optional if you are using unflavored collagen powder)

Direction:

Line a 9-inch square baking pan with parchment paper.

In a food processor or blender, combine the pili nuts, hazelnuts, walnuts, sunflower seeds, coconut, hemp seeds, cacao nibs, collagen powder, cinnamon, and salt and pulse a few times.

Add the coconut oil, vanilla extract, and sweetener (if using). Pulse again until the ingredients are combined. Do not over pulse or it will turn to mush. You want the nuts and seeds to have some texture still.

Pour the mixture into the prepared pan and press it into an even layer. Cover with another piece of parchment (or fold over extra from the first piece) and place a heavy pot or dish on top to help press the bars together.

Refrigerate overnight and then cut into 12 bars. Store the bars in individual storage bags in the refrigerator for a quick grab-and-go breakfast.

Nutrition:

Calories: 242

Total Fat: 22g

Protein: 6.5g

Total Carbs: 4.5g

Fiber: 2.5g - Net Carbs: 2g

Easy Skillet Pancakes

Preparation Time: 5 minutes

Cooking time: 5 minutes

Servings: 8

Ingredients:

8 ounces cream cheese

8 eggs

2 tablespoons coconut flour

2 teaspoons baking powder

1 teaspoon ground cinnamon

½ teaspoon vanilla extract

1 teaspoon liquid stevia or sweetener of choice (optional)

2 tablespoons butter

Directions

In a blender, combine the cream cheese, eggs, coconut flour, baking powder, cinnamon, vanilla, and stevia (if using). Blend until smooth.

In a large skillet over medium heat, melt the butter.

Use half the mixture to pour four evenly sized pancakes and cook for about a minute, until you see bubbles on top. Flip the pancakes and cook for another minute. Remove from the pan and add more butter or oil to the skillet if needed. Repeat with the remaining batter.

Top with butter and eat right away, or freeze the pancakes in a freezer-safe resealable bag with sheets of parchment in between, for up to 1 month.

Nutrition:

Calories: 179 - Total Fat: 15g - Protein: 8g

Total Carbs: 3g - Fiber: 1g - Net Carbs: 2g

Quick Keto Blender Muffins

Preparation Time: 5 minutes

Cooking time: 25 minutes

Servings: 12

Ingredients

Butter, ghee, or coconut oil for greasing the pan

6 eggs

8 ounces cream cheese, at room temperature

2 scoops flavored collagen powder

1 teaspoon ground cinnamon

1 teaspoon baking powder

Few drops or dash sweetener (optional)

Directions:

Preheat the oven to 350°F. Grease a 12-cup muffin pan very well with butter, ghee, or coconut oil. Alternatively, you can use silicone cups or paper muffin liners.

In a blender, combine the eggs, cream cheese, collagen powder, cinnamon, baking powder, and sweetener (if using). Blend until well combined and pour the mixture into the muffin cups, dividing equally.

Bake for 22 to 25 minutes until the muffins are golden brown on top and firm.

Let cool then store in a glass container or plastic bag in the refrigerator for up to 2 weeks or in the freezer for up to 3 months.

To servings refrigerated muffins, heat in the microwave for 30 seconds. To meals from frozen, thaw in the refrigerator overnight and then microwave for 30 seconds, or microwave straight from the freezer for 45 to 60 seconds or until heated through.

Nutrition:

Calories: 120

Total Fat: 10g

Protein: 6g

Total Carbs: 1.5g

Fiber: 0g

Net Carbs: 1.5g

Keto Everything Bagels
Preparation Time: 10 minutes

Cooking time: 15 minutes

Servings: 8

Ingredients:

2 cups shredded mozzarella cheese

2 tablespoons labneh cheese (or cream cheese)

1½ cups almond flour

1 egg

2 teaspoons baking powder

¼ teaspoon sea salt

1 tablespoon Everything Seasoning

Directions

Preheat the oven to 400°F.

In a microwave-safe bowl, combine the mozzarella and labneh cheeses. Microwave for 30 seconds, stir, then microwave for another 30 seconds. Stir well. If not melted completely, microwave for another 10 to 20 seconds.

Add the almond flour, egg, baking powder, and salt to the bowl and mix well. Form into a dough using a spatula or your hands.

Cut the dough into 8 roughly equal pieces and form into balls.

Roll each dough ball into a cylinder, then pinch the ends together to seal.

Place the dough rings in a nonstick donut pan or arrange them on a parchment paper–lined baking sheet.

Sprinkle with the seasoning and bake for 12 to 15 minutes or until golden brown.

Store in plastic bags in the freezer and defrost overnight in the refrigerator. Reheat in the oven or toaster for a quick grab-and-go breakfast.

Nutrition:

Calories: 241- Total Fat: 19g - Protein: 12g - Total Carbs: 5.5g - Fiber: 2.5g - Net Carbs: 3g

Turmeric Chicken and Kale Salad with Food, Lemon and Honey

Preparation Time: 20 minutes

Cooking time: 15 minutes

Servings: 4

Ingredients:

For the chicken:

1 teaspoon of clarified butter or 1 tablespoon of coconut oil

½ medium brown onion, diced

250-300 g / 9 ounces minced chicken meat or diced chicken legs

1 large garlic clove, diced

1 teaspoon of turmeric powder

1 teaspoon of lime zest

½ lime juice

½ teaspoon of salt + pepper

For the salad:

6 stalks of broccoli or 2 cups of broccoli flowers

2 tablespoons of pumpkin seeds (seeds)

3 large cabbage leaves, stems removed and chopped

½ sliced avocado

Handful of fresh coriander leaves, chopped

Handful of fresh parsley leaves, chopped

For the dressing:

3 tablespoons of lime juice

1 small garlic clove, diced or grated

3 tablespoons of virgin olive oil (I used 1 tablespoon of avocado oil and 2 tablespoons of EVO)

1 teaspoon of raw honey

½ teaspoon whole or Dijon mustard

½ teaspoon of sea salt with pepper

Directions:

Heat the coconut oil in a pan. Add the onion and sauté over medium heat for 4-5 minutes, until golden brown. Add the minced chicken and garlic and stir 2-3 minutes over medium-high heat, separating.

Add your turmeric, lime zest, lime juice, salt and pepper, and cook, stirring consistently, for another 3-4 minutes. Set the ground beef aside.

While your chicken is cooking, put a small saucepan of water to the boil. Add your broccoli and cook for 2 minutes. Rinse with cold water and cut into 3-4 pieces each.

Add the pumpkin seeds to the chicken pan and toast over medium heat for 2 minutes, frequently stirring to avoid burning. Season with a little salt. Set aside. Raw pumpkin seeds are also good to use. Put the chopped cabbage in a salad bowl and pour it over the dressing. Using your hands, mix, and massage the cabbage with the dressing. This will soften the cabbage, a bit like citrus juice with fish or beef Carpaccio: it "cooks" it a little. Finally, mix the cooked chicken, broccoli, fresh herbs, pumpkin seeds, and avocado slices.

Nutrition:

232 calories Fat 11 Fiber 9

Carbs 8 Protein 14

Buckwheat Spaghetti with Chicken Cabbage and Savory Food Recipes in Mass Sauce

Preparation Time: 15 minutes

Cooking time: 15 minutes'

Servings: 2

Ingredients:

For the noodles:

2-3 handfuls of cabbage leaves (removed from the stem and cut)

Buckwheat noodles 150g / 5oz (100% buckwheat, without wheat)

3-4 shiitake mushrooms, sliced

1 teaspoon of coconut oil or butter

1 brown onion, finely chopped

1 medium chicken breast, sliced or diced

1 long red pepper, thinly sliced (seeds in or out depending on how hot you like it)

2 large garlic cloves, diced

2-3 tablespoons of Tamari sauce (gluten-free soy sauce)

For the miso dressing:

1 tablespoon and a half of fresh organic miso

1 tablespoon of Tamari sauce

1 tablespoon of extra virgin olive oil

1 tablespoon of lemon or lime juice

1 teaspoon of sesame oil (optional)

Directions:

Boil a medium saucepan of water. Add the black cabbage and cook 1 minute, until it is wilted. Remove and reserve, but reserve the water and return to boiling. Add your soba noodles and cook according to the directions on the package (usually about 5 minutes). Rinse with cold water and reserve.

In the meantime, fry the shiitake mushrooms in a little butter or coconut oil (about a teaspoon) for 2-3 minutes, until its color is lightly browned on each side. Sprinkle with sea salt and reserve.

In that same pan, heat more coconut oil or lard over medium-high heat. Fry the onion and chili for 2-3 minutes, and then add the chicken pieces. Cook 5 minutes on medium heat, stirring a few times, then add the garlic, tamari sauce, and a little water. Cook for another 2-3 minutes, stirring continuously until your chicken is cooked.

Finally, add the cabbage and soba noodles and stir the chicken to warm it.

Stir the miso sauce and sprinkle the noodles at the end of the cooking, in this way you will keep alive all the beneficial probiotics in the miso.

Nutrition:

305 calories Fat 11

Fiber 7 Carbs 9 Protein 12

Asian King Jumped Jamp

Preparation Time: 15 minutes

Cooking time: 10 minutes

Servings: 4

Ingredients:

150 g / 5 oz. of raw shelled prawns, not chopped

Two teaspoons of tamari (you can use soy sauce if you don't avoid gluten)

Two teaspoons of extra virgin olive oil

75 g / 2.6 oz. soba (buckwheat pasta) - 1 garlic clove, finely chopped

1 bird's eye chili, finely chopped - 1 teaspoon finely chopped fresh ginger.

20 g / 0.7 oz. of sliced red onions

40 g / 1.4 oz. of celery, cut and sliced

75 g / 2.6 oz. of chopped green beans

50 g / 1.7 oz. of chopped cabbage

100 ml / ½ cup of chicken broth

5 g celery or celery leaves

Directions:

Heat a pan over high heat, and then cook the prawns in 1 teaspoon of tamari and 1 teaspoon of oil for 2-3 minutes. Transfer the prawns to a plate. Clean the pan with kitchen paper as it will be reused.

Cook your noodles in boiling water for 5-8 minutes or as indicated on the package. Drain and set aside.

Meanwhile, fry the garlic, chili and ginger, red onion, celery, beans, and cabbage in the remaining oil over medium-high heat for 2-3 minutes. Add your broth and allow it to boil, and then simmer for a minute or two, until the vegetables are cooked but crunchy.

Add shrimp, noodles and celery/celery leaves to the pan, bring to a boil again, then remove from the heat and serve.

Nutrition:

Calories 223 - Protein 34 - Fat 2 - Carbs 6

Buckwheat Pasta Salad

Preparation Time: 10 minutes

Cooking time: 30 minutes

Servings: 4

Ingredients:

50 g / 1.7 oz. buckwheat pasta

Large handful of rockets

A small handful of basil leaves

Eight cherry tomatoes halved

1/2 avocado, diced

Ten olives

1 tablespoon. extra olive virgin oil

20 g / 0.70 oz. pine nuts

Directions:

Combine all the ingredients except your pine nuts. Arrange your combination on a plate, and then scatter the pine nuts over the top.

Nutrition:

125 calories - Fat 6 - Fiber 5 - Carbs 10 - Protein 11

Greek Salad Skewers

Preparation Time: 35 minutes

Cooking time: 0 minutes

Servings: 2

Ingredients:

Two wooden skewers, soaked in water for 30 minutes before use

Eight large black olives

Eight cherry tomatoes

1 yellow pepper, cut into eight squares.

½ red onions, you can cut in half and separated into eight pieces

100 g / 3.5 oz. (about 10cm) cucumber, cut into four slices and halved

100 g / 3.5 oz. feta, cut into eight cubes

For the dressing:

1 tablespoon. extra olive virgin oil

Juice of ½ lemons

1 teaspoon. of your balsamic vinegar

½ clove garlic, ensure it peeled and crushed

Basil leaves chopped (or ½ teaspoon. dried mixed herbs to replace basil and oregano)

Oregano leaves,

Salt and grounded black pepper

Directions:

Blend each skewer with the salad ingredients in the order

Put all your dressing ingredients into a bowl and mix thoroughly. Pour over the skewers.

Nutrition:

Calories 99

Protein 34

Fat 4 - Carbs 5

Kale, Edamame and Tofu Curry

Preparation Time: 20 minutes

Cooking time: 40 minutes

Servings: 3

Ingredients:

1 tablespoon rapeseed oil

1 large onion, chopped

Four cloves garlic, peeled and grated

1 large thumb (7cm) fresh ginger, peeled and grated

1 red chili, deseeded and thinly sliced

1/2 teaspoon ground turmeric

1/4 teaspoon cayenne pepper

1 teaspoon paprika

1/2 teaspoon ground cumin

1 teaspoon salt

250 g / 9 oz. dried red lentils

1-liter boiling water

50 g / 1.7 oz. frozen soya beans

200 g / 7 oz. firm tofu, chopped into cubes

Two tomatoes, roughly chopped

Juice of 1 lime

200 g / 7 oz. kale leaves stalk removed and torn

Directions:

Put the oil in a pan over low heat. Add your onion and cook for 5 minutes before adding the garlic, ginger, and chili and cooking for a further 2 minutes. Add your turmeric, cayenne, paprika, cumin, and salt and Stir through before adding the red lentils and stirring again.

Pour in the boiling water and allow it to simmer for 10 minutes, reduce the heat and cook for about 20-30 minutes until the curry has a thick '•porridge' consistency.

Add your tomatoes, tofu and soya beans and cook for a further 5 minutes. Add your kale leaves and lime juice and cook until the kale is just tender.

Nutrition:

Calories 133 Carbohydrate 54

Protein 43

Chocolate Cupcakes with Matcha Icing

Preparation Time: 35 minutes

Cooking time: 0 minutes

Servings: 4

Ingredients:

150g / 5 oz. self-rising flour

200 g / 7 oz. caster sugar

60 g / 2.1 oz. cocoa

½ teaspoon. salt

½ teaspoon. fine espresso coffee, decaf if preferred

120 ml / ½ cup milk

½ teaspoon. vanilla extract

50 ml / ¼ cup vegetable oil

1 egg

120 ml / ½ cup of water

For the icing:

50 g / 1.7 oz. butter,

50 g / 1.7 oz. icing sugar

1 tablespoon matcha green tea powder

½ teaspoon vanilla bean paste

50 g / 1.7 oz. soft cream cheese

Directions:

Heat the oven and Line a cupcake tin with paper

Put the flour, sugar, cocoa, salt, and coffee powder in a large bowl and mix well.

Add milk, vanilla extract, vegetable oil, and egg to dry ingredients and use an electric mixer to beat until well combined. Gently pour the boiling water slowly and beat on low speed until thoroughly combined. Use the high speed to beat for another minute to add air to the dough. The dough is much more liquid than a standard cake mix. Have faith; It will taste fantastic! Arrange the dough evenly between the cake boxes. Each cake box must not be more than ¾ full. Bake for 15-18 minutes, until the mixture resumes when hit. Remove from oven and allow cooling completely before icing. To make the icing, beat your butter and icing sugar until they turn pale and smooth. Add the matcha powder and vanilla and mix again. Add the cream cheese and beat until it is smooth. Pipe or spread on the cakes.

Nutrition:

calories435 Fat 5 Fiber 3

Carbs 7 Protein 9

Sesame Chicken Salad

Preparation Time: 20 minutes

Cooking time: 0 minutes

Servings: 4

Ingredients:

1 tablespoon of sesame seeds

1 cucumber, peeled, halved lengthwise, without a teaspoon, and sliced.

100 g / 3.5 oz. cabbage, chopped

60 g pak choi, finely chopped

½ red onion, thinly sliced

Large parsley (20 g / 0.7 oz.), chopped.

150 g / 5 oz. cooked chicken, minced

For the dressing:

1 tablespoon of extra virgin olive oil

1 teaspoon of sesame oil

1 lime juice

1 teaspoon of light honey

2 teaspoons soy sauce

Directions:

Roast your sesame seeds in a dry pan for 2 minutes until they become slightly golden and fragrant.

Transfer to a plate to cool.

In a small bowl, mix olive oil, sesame oil, lime juice, honey, and soy sauce to prepare the dressing. Place the cucumber, black cabbage, pak choi, red onion, and parsley in a large bowl and mix gently. Pour over the dressing and mix again.

Distribute the salad between two dishes and complete with the shredded chicken. Sprinkle with sesame seeds just before serving.

Nutrition:

Calories 345 Fat 5 Fiber 2 Carbs 10

Protein 4

Bacon Appetizers

Preparation Time: 15 minutes

Cooking Time: 2 hours

Servings: 6

Ingredients:

1 pack Keto crackers

¾ cup Parmesan cheese, grated

1 lb. bacon, sliced thinly

Directions:

Preheat your oven to 250 degrees F. Arrange the crackers on a baking sheet. Sprinkle cheese on top of each cracker. Wrap each cracker with the bacon. Bake in the oven for 2 hours.

Nutrition:

Calories 440 Total Fat 33.4g

Saturated Fat 11g Cholesterol 86mg

Sodium 1813mg Total Carbohydrate 3.7g

Dietary Fiber 0.1g Total Sugars 0.1g

Protein 29.4g Potassium 432mg

Antipasti Skewers

Preparation Time: 10 minutes

Cooking Time: 0 minute

Servings: 6

Ingredients:

6 small mozzarella balls

1 tablespoon olive oil

Salt to taste

1/8 teaspoon dried oregano

2 roasted yellow peppers, sliced into strips and rolled

6 cherry tomatoes - 6 green olives, pitted

6 Kalamata olives, pitted

2 artichoke hearts, sliced into wedges

6 slices salami, rolled - 6 leaves fresh basil

Directions:

Toss the mozzarella balls in olive oil. Season with salt and oregano. Thread the mozzarella balls and the rest of the ingredients into skewers. Serve in a platter.

Nutrition:

Calories 180 - Total Fat 11.8g Saturated Fat 4.5g - Cholesterol 26mg Sodium 482mg - Total Carbohydrate 11.7g Dietary Fiber 4.8g - Total Sugars 4.1g Protein 9.2g - Potassium 538mg

Jalapeno Poppers

Preparation Time: 30 minutes

Cooking Time: 60 minutes

Servings: 10

Ingredients:

5 fresh jalapenos, sliced and seeded

4 oz. package cream cheese

¼ lb. bacon, sliced in half

Directions:

Preheat your oven to 275 degrees F. Place a wire rack over your baking sheet. Stuff each jalapeno with cream cheese and wrap in bacon. Secure with a toothpick. Place on the baking sheet.

Bake for 1 hour and 15 minutes.

Nutrition: Calories 103 - Total Fat 8.7g - Saturated Fat 4.1g

Cholesterol 25mg - Sodium 296mg - Total Carbohydrate 0.9g

Dietary Fiber 0.2g - Total Sugars 0.3g - Protein 5.2g - Potassium 93mg

BLT Party Bites

Preparation Time: 35 minutes

Cooking Time: 0 minute

Servings: 8

Ingredients:

4 oz. bacon, chopped - 3 tablespoons panko breadcrumbs

1 tablespoon Parmesan cheese, grated - 1 teaspoon mayonnaise

1 teaspoon lemon juice - Salt to taste

½ heart Romaine lettuce, shredded

6 cocktail tomatoes

Directions:

Put the bacon in a pan over medium heat.

Fry until crispy. Transfer bacon to a plate lined with paper towel. Add breadcrumbs and cook until crunchy. Transfer breadcrumbs to another plate also lined with paper towel. Sprinkle Parmesan cheese on top of the breadcrumbs. Mix the mayonnaise, salt and lemon juice. Toss the Romaine in the mayo mixture. Slice each tomato on the bottom to create a flat surface so it can stand by itself. Slice the top off as well. Scoop out the insides of the tomatoes.

Stuff each tomato with the bacon, Parmesan, breadcrumbs and top with the lettuce.

Nutrition:

Calories 107 - Total Fat 6.5g - Saturated Fat 2.1g - Cholesterol 16mg - Sodium 360mg

Total Carbohydrate 5.4g - Dietary Fiber 1.5g - Total Sugars 3.3g - Protein 6.5g

Potassium 372mg

Eggs Benedict Deviled Eggs

Preparation Time: 15 minutes

Cooking Time: 25 minutes

Servings: 16

Ingredients:

8 hardboiled eggs, sliced in half

1 tablespoon lemon juice

½ teaspoon mustard powder

1 pack Hollandaise sauce mix, prepared according to direction in the packaging

1 lb. asparagus, trimmed and steamed

4 oz. bacon, cooked and chopped

Directions:

Scoop out the egg yolks.

Mix the egg yolks with lemon juice, mustard powder and 1/3 cup of the Hollandaise sauce.

Spoon the egg yolk mixture into each of the egg whites.

Arrange the asparagus spears on a serving plate. Top with the deviled eggs.

Sprinkle remaining sauce and bacon on top.

Nutrition:

Calories 80 Total Fat 5.3g

Saturated Fat 1.7g Cholesterol 90mg

Sodium 223mg Total Carbohydrate 2.1g

Dietary Fiber 0.6g Total Sugars 0.7g

Protein 6.2g Potassium 133mg

Spinach Meatballs
Preparation Time: 20 minutes

Cooking Time: 30 minutes

Servings: 4

Ingredients:

1 cup spinach, chopped - 1 ½ lb. ground turkey breast

1 onion, chopped

3 cloves garlic, minced

1 egg, beaten

¼ cup milk

¾ cup breadcrumbs

½ cup Parmesan cheese, grated

Salt and pepper to taste

2 tablespoons butter

2 tablespoons Keto flour

10 oz. Italian cheese, shredded

½ teaspoon nutmeg, freshly grated

¼ cup parsley, chopped

Directions:

Preheat your oven to 400 degrees F. Mix all the ingredients in a large bowl. Form meatballs from the mixture. Bake in the oven for 20 minutes.

Nutrition:

Calories 374 Total Fat 18.5g Saturated Fat 10g Cholesterol 118mg Sodium 396mg

Total Carbohydrate 11.3g Dietary Fiber 1g Total Sugars 1.7g

Protein 34.2g Potassium 336mg

Bacon Wrapped Asparagus
Preparation Time: 10 minutes

Cooking Time: 20 minutes

Servings: 6

Ingredients:

1 ½ lb. asparagus spears, sliced in half

6 slices bacon

2 tablespoons olive oil

Salt and pepper to taste

Directions:

Preheat your oven to 400 degrees F. Wrap a handful of asparagus with bacon. Secure with a toothpick. Drizzle with the olive oil. Season with salt and pepper. Bake in the oven for 20 minutes or until bacon is crispy.

Nutrition:

Calories 166 Total Fat 12.8g

Saturated Fat 3.3g Cholesterol 21mg

Sodium 441mg Total Carbohydrate 4.7g

Dietary Fiber 2.4g Total Sugars 2.1g

Protein 9.5g Potassium 337mg

Kale Chips

Preparation Time: 5 minutes

Cooking Time: 12 minutes

Servings: 2

Ingredients:

1 bunch kale, removed from the stems

2 tablespoons extra virgin olive oil

1 tablespoon garlic salt

Directions:

Preheat your oven to 350 degrees F.

Coat the kale with olive oil.

Arrange on a baking sheet.

Bake for 12 minutes.

Sprinkle with garlic salt.

Nutrition:

Calories 100 Total Fat 7g 9% Saturated Fat 1g 5% Cholesterol 0mg 0%

Sodium 30mg 1% Total Carbohydrate 8.5g 3% Dietary Fiber 1.2g 4% Total Sugars 0.5g

Protein 2.4g Calcium 92mg 7% Iron 1mg 6% Potassium 352mg

Bacon, Mozzarella & Avocado

Preparation Time: 15 minutes

Cooking Time: 15 minutes

Servings: 2

Ingredients:

3 slices bacon

1 cup mozzarella cheese, shredded

6 eggs, beaten

2 tablespoons butter

½ avocado

1 oz. cheddar cheese, shredded

Salt and pepper to taste

Directions:

Fry the bacon in a pan until crispy.

Transfer to a plate and set aside.

Place the mozzarella cheese the pan and cook until the edges have browned.

Cook the eggs in butter.

Stuff mozzarella with scrambled eggs, bacon and mashed avocado. Sprinkle cheese on top. Season with salt and pepper.

Nutrition:

Calories 645

Total Fat 53.6g Saturated Fat 21.9g

Cholesterol 575mg Sodium 1101mg

Total Carbohydrate 6.5g Dietary Fiber 3.4g

Total Sugars 1.4g Protein 35.8g

Potassium 600mg

Keto Cheese Chips

Preparation Time: 10 minutes

Cooking Time: 10 minutes

Servings: 3

Ingredients:

1 ½ cups cheddar cheese, shredded

3 tablespoons ground flaxseed meal

Garlic salt to taste

Directions:

Preheat your oven to 425 degrees F.

Create a small pile of 2 tablespoons cheddar cheese on a baking sheet.

Sprinkle flaxseed on top of each chip.

Season with garlic salt.

Bake in the oven for 10 minutes.

Let cool before serving.

Nutrition:

Calories 288 Total Fat 22.2g Saturated Fat 11.9g Cholesterol 59mg Sodium 356mg

Total Carbohydrate 5.8g Dietary Fiber 4g Total Sugars 0.3g Protein 17.1g Potassium 57mg

Beef & Broccoli

Preparation Time: 10 minutes

Cooking Time: 15 minutes

Servings: 2

Ingredients:

¼ cup coconut amino, divided

1 teaspoon garlic, minced and divided

1 teaspoon fresh ginger, minced and divided

8 oz. beef, sliced thinly

1 ½ tablespoon avocado oil, divided

2 ½ cups broccolis, sliced into florets

¼ cup low sodium beef stock

½ teaspoon sesame oil

Salt to taste

Sesame seeds

Green onion, chopped

Directions:

In a bowl, mix the one tablespoon coconut amino with half of the ginger and garlic.

Marinate the beef into this mixture for 1 hour.

Cover with foil and place in the refrigerator.

Put 1 tablespoon oil in a pan over medium heat.

Add the broccoli and cook for 3 minutes.

Add the remaining ginger and garlic.

Cook for 1 minute.

Reduce the heat.

Cover the pan with its lid.

Cook until the broccoli is tender but still a little crunchy.

Transfer the broccoli to a platter.

Increase the heat and add the remaining oil.

Add the beef and cook for 3 minutes.

Put the broccoli back.

In a bowl, mix the remaining coconut amino, broth and sesame oil.

Pour into the pan.

Cook until the sauce has thickened.

Season with salt.

Garnish with sesame seeds and green onion.

Nutrition:

Calories 298 Total Fat 10g Saturated Fat 3.1g

Cholesterol 101mg Sodium 1989mg

Total Carbohydrate 12.2g Dietary Fiber 4g

Total Sugars 2.7g Protein 40g Potassium 958mg

Beef Stroganoff

Preparation Time: 20 minutes

Cooking Time: 2 hours and 10 minutes

Servings: 10

Ingredients:

¼ cup avocado oil

1 white onion, chopped

2 teaspoons garlic, minced

3 lb. beef brisket, fat trimmed and sliced into bite size pieces

Salt and pepper to taste

2 teaspoons ground thyme

1 ½ cups beef broth

2 tablespoons apple cider vinegar

16 oz. fresh mushrooms, sliced

¾ cup sour cream

¼ cup mayonnaise

1 ½ teaspoon xanthan gum

Directions:

Place your pan over medium heat.

Add the oil, onion and garlic.

Sauté for 3 minutes.

Add the beef.

Season with salt, pepper and thyme.

Cook for 8 minutes, stirring frequently.

Reduce heat and add beef broth and vinegar.

Simmer for 30 minutes.

Add mushrooms and cover the pan.

Simmer for 1 hour and 30 minutes.

Remove the pan from the stove.

Stir in the mayonnaise and sour cream.

Gradually stir in the xanthan gum until the sauce has thickened.

Cover the pan and let sit for 10 minutes before serving.

Nutrition:

Calories 343

Total Fat 15.1g

Saturated Fat 6g

Cholesterol 131mg

Sodium 292mg Total Carbohydrate 6.5g

Dietary Fiber 2g

Total Sugars 1.8g

Protein 44.4g

Potassium 789mg

Garlic Butter Steak

Preparation Time: 10 minutes

Cooking Time: 15 minutes

Servings: 2

Ingredients:

2 rib eye steaks, trimmed

1 ½ tablespoons olive oil, divided

Salt and pepper to taste

2 tablespoons butter

2 cloves garlic, minced

2 sprigs fresh rosemary, chopped

Directions:

Dry the steaks using a paper towel.

Put a cast iron skillet over high heat.

Wait until the skillet starts to smoke.

Add 1 tablespoon oil to the skillet.

Coat the steaks with the remaining oil.

Season steaks with salt and pepper.

Add the steaks to the hot pan.

Sear for 5 to 7 minutes for medium and up to 10 minutes for medium well.

Reduce the heat to low.

Add the butter, garlic and the rosemary.

Cook for another minute.

Let the steak rest for before slicing and serving.

Nutrition:

Calories 547

Total Fat 48.1g

Saturated Fat 19.3g

Cholesterol 120mg

Sodium 142mg

Total Carbohydrate 1.2g

Dietary Fiber 0.4g

Total Sugars 0g

Protein 26.9g

Potassium 18mg

Beef Shawarma

Preparation Time: 5 minutes

Cooking Time: 15 minutes

Servings: 4

Ingredients:

2 tablespoons olive oil

1 lb. lean ground beef

1 cup onion, sliced

Salt to taste

3 tablespoons shawarma mix

3 cups cabbage, shredded

2 tablespoons water

1/4 cup parsley, chopped

Directions:

Put your pan over medium heat.

Once the pan starts to sizzle, add the olive oil.

Add the ground beef.

Add the onion and cook for 4 minutes.

Season with salt and shawarma mix.

Add the cabbage.

Pour in the water.

Cover the pan and steam for 1 minute.

Garnish with parsley before serving.

Nutrition:

Calories 330 Total Fat 15.3g

Saturated Fat 4.1g

Cholesterol 101mg

Sodium 201mg

Total Carbohydrate 12g

Dietary Fiber 4.3g

Total Sugars 2.9g

Protein 35.9g Potassium 609mg

CHAPTER 10:

Lunch Recipes

Chicken, Bacon and Avocado Cloud Sandwiches

Preparation Time: 10 minutes

Cooking time: 25 minutes

Servings: 6

Ingredients:

For cloud bread

3 large eggs

4 oz. cream cheese

½ tablespoon. ground psyllium husk powder

½ teaspoon baking powder

A pinch of salt

To assemble sandwich

6 slices of bacon, cooked and chopped

6 slices pepper Jack cheese

½ avocado, sliced

1 cup cooked chicken breasts, shredded

3 tablespoons. mayonnaise

Directions:

Preheat your oven to 300 degrees.

Prepare a baking sheet by lining it with parchment paper.

Separate the egg whites and egg yolks, and place into separate bowls.

Whisk the egg whites until very stiff. Set aside.

Combined egg yolks and cream cheese.

Add the psyllium husk powder and baking powder to the egg yolk mixture. Gently fold in. Add the egg whites into the egg mixture and gently fold in. Dollop the mixture onto the prepared baking sheet to create 12 cloud bread. Use a spatula to spread the circles around to form ½-inch thick pieces gently.

Bake for 25 minutes or until the tops are golden brown.

Allow the cloud bread to cool completely before serving. Can be refrigerated for up to 3 days of frozen for up to 3 months. If food prepping, place a layer of parchment paper between each bread slice to avoid having them getting stuck together. Simply toast in the oven for 5 minutes when it is time to servings.

To assemble sandwiches, place mayonnaise on one side of one cloud bread. Layer with the remaining sandwich ingredients and top with another slice of cloud bread. Servings.

Nutrition:

Calories: 333 kcal Carbs: 5g

Fat: 26g Protein: 19.9g

Roasted Lemon Chicken Sandwich

Preparation Time: 15 minutes

Cooking time: 1 hour 30 minutes

Servings: 12

Ingredients:

1 kg whole chicken

5 tablespoons. butter

1 lemon, cut into wedges

1 tablespoon. garlic powder

Salt and pepper to taste

2 tablespoons. mayonnaise

Keto-friendly bread

Directions:

Preheat the oven to 350 degrees F.

Grease a deep baking dish with butter.

Ensure that the chicken is patted dry and that the gizzards have been removed.

Combine the butter, garlic powder, salt and pepper.

Rub the entire chicken with it, including in the cavity.

Place the lemon and onion inside the chicken and place the chicken in the prepared baking dish.

Bake for about 1½ hours, depending on the size of the chicken.

Baste the chicken often with the drippings. If the drippings begin to dry, add water. The chicken is done when a thermometer, insert it into the thickest part of the thigh reads 165 degrees F or when the clear juices run when the thickest part of the thigh is pierced.

Allow the chicken to cool before slicing.

To assemble sandwich, shred some of the breast meat and mix with the mayonnaise. Place the mixture between the two bread slices.

To save the chicken, refrigerated for up to 5 days or freeze for up to 1 month.

Nutrition:

Calories: 214 kcal Carbs: 1.6 g

Fat: 11.8 g Protein: 24.4 g.

Keto-Friendly Skillet Pepperoni Pizza

Preparation Time: 10 minutes

Cooking time: 6 minutes

Servings: 4

Ingredients:

For Crust

½ cup almond flour

½ teaspoon baking powder

8 large egg whites, whisked into stiff peaks

Salt and pepper to taste

Toppings

3 tablespoons. unsweetened tomato sauce

½ cup shredded cheddar cheese

½ cup pepperoni

Directions

Gently incorporate the almond flour into the egg whites. Ensure that no lumps remain. Stir in the remaining crust ingredients. Heat a nonstick skillet over medium heat. Spray with nonstick spray. Pour the batter into the heated skillet to cover the bottom of the skillet. Cover the skillet with a lid and cook the pizza crust to cook for about 4 minutes or until bubbles that appear on the top. Flip the dough and add the toppings, starting with the tomato sauce and ending with the pepperoni Cook the pizza for 2 more minutes. Allow the pizza to cool slightly before serving. Can be stored in the refrigerator for up to 5 days and frozen for up to 1 month.

Nutrition:

Calories: 175 kcal - Carbs: 1.9 g

Fat: 12 g - Protein: 14.3 g.

Cheesy Chicken Cauliflower

Preparation Time: 5 minutes

Cooking time: 10 minutes

Servings: 4

Ingredients:

2 cups cauliflower florets, chopped

½ cup red bell pepper, chopped

1 cup roasted chicken, shredded (Lunch Recipes: Roasted Lemon Chicken Sandwich)

¼ cup shredded cheddar cheese

1 tablespoon. butter

1 tablespoon. sour cream

Salt and pepper to taste

Directions:

Stir fry the cauliflower and peppers in the butter over medium heat until the veggies are tender.

Add the chicken and cook until the chicken is warmed through.

Add the remaining ingredients and stir until the cheese is melted.

serve warm.

Nutrition:

Calories: 144 kcal Carbs: 4 g

Fat: 8.5 g Protein: 13.2 g.

Chicken Soup

Preparation Time: 10 minutes

Cooking time: 25 minutes

Servings: 6

Ingredients:

4 cups roasted chicken, shredded (Lunch Recipes: Roasted Lemon Chicken Sandwich)

2 tablespoons. butter

2 celery stalks, chopped

1 cup mushrooms, sliced

4 cups green cabbage, sliced into strips

2 garlic cloves, minced

6 cups chicken broth

1 carrot, sliced

Salt and pepper to taste

1 tablespoon. garlic powder

1 tablespoon. onion powder

Directions:

Sauté the celery, mushrooms and garlic in the butter in a pot over medium heat for 4 minutes. Add broth, carrots, garlic powder, onion powder, salt, and pepper. Simmer for 10 minutes or until the vegetables are tender. Add the chicken and cabbage and simmer for another 10 minutes or until the cabbage is tender. Servings warm. Can be refrigerated for up to 3 days or frozen for up to 1 month.

Nutrition:

Calories: 279 kcal Carbs: 7.5 g Fat: 12.3 g

Protein: 33.4 g.

Chicken Avocado Salad

Preparation Time: 7 minutes

Cooking time: 10 minutes

Servings: 4

Ingredients:

1 cup roasted chicken, shredded (Lunch Recipes: Roasted Lemon Chicken Sandwich)

1 bacon strip, cooked and chopped - 1/2 medium avocado, chopped

¼ cup cheddar cheese, grated

1 hard-boiled egg, chopped

1 cup romaine lettuce, chopped

1 tablespoon. olive oil

1 tablespoon. apple cider vinegar

Salt and pepper to taste

Directions:

Create the dressing by mixing apple cider vinegar, oil, salt and pepper.

Combine all the other ingredients in a mixing bowl.

Drizzle with the dressing and toss. Servings.

Can be refrigerated for up to 3 days.

Nutrition:

Calories: 220 kcal - Carbs: 2.8 g - Fat: 16.7 g - Protein: 14.8 g.

Chicken Broccoli Dinner

Preparation Time: 10 minutes

Cooking time: 5 minutes

Servings: 1

Ingredients:

1 roasted chicken leg (Lunch Recipes: Roasted Lemon Chicken Sandwich)

½ cup broccoli florets

½ tablespoon. unsalted butter, softened

2 garlic cloves, minced

Salt and pepper to taste

Directions:

Boil the broccoli in lightly salted water for 5 minutes. Drain the water from the pot and keep the broccoli in the pot. Keep the lid on to keep the broccoli warm.

Mix all the butter, garlic, salt and pepper in a small bowl to create garlic butter.

Place the chicken, broccoli and garlic butter. Servings.

Nutrition:

Calories: 257 kcal Carbs: 5.1 g

Fat: 14 g - Protein: 27.4 g.

Easy Meatballs
Preparation Time: 10 minutes

Cooking time: 20 minutes

 Servings: 4

Ingredients:

1 lb. ground beef

1 egg, beaten

Salt and pepper to taste

1 teaspoon garlic powder

1 teaspoon onion powder

2 tablespoons. butter

¼ cup mayonnaise

¼ cup pickled jalapeños

1 cup cheddar cheese, grated

Directions

Combine the cheese, mayonnaise, pickled jalapenos, salt, pepper, garlic powder and onion powder in a large mixing bowl. Add the beef and egg and combine using clean hands. Form large meatballs. Makes about 12. Fry the meatballs in the butter over medium heat for about 4 minutes on each side or until golden brown. Servings warm with a keto-friendly side. The meatball mixture can also be used to make a meatloaf. Just preheat your oven to 400 degrees F, press the mixture into a loaf pan and bake for about 30 minutes or until the top is golden brown. Can be refrigerated for up to 5 days or frozen for up to 3 months.

Nutrition:

Calories: 454 kcal Carbs: 5 g - Fat: 28.2 g

Protein: 43.2 g.

Chicken Casserole
Preparation Time: 10 minutes

Cooking time: 40 minutes

Servings: 8

Ingredients:

1 lb. boneless chicken breasts, cut into 1" cubes

2 tablespoons. butter

4 tablespoons. green pesto

1 cup heavy whipping cream

¼ cup green bell peppers, diced

1 cup feta cheese, diced

1 garlic clove, minced

Salt and pepper to taste

Directions

Preheat your oven to 400 degrees F. Season the chicken with salt and pepper then batch fry in the butter until golden brown. Place the fried chicken pieces in a baking dish. Add the feta cheese, garlic and bell peppers. Combine the pesto and heavy cream in a bowl. Pour on top of the chicken mixture and spread with a spatula. Bake for 30 minutes or until the casserole is light brown around the edges. Servings warm. Can be refrigerated for up to 5 days and frozen for 2 weeks.

Nutrition:

Calories: 294 kcal Carbs: 1.7 g Fat: 22.7 g

Protein: 20.1 g.

Lemon Baked Salmon

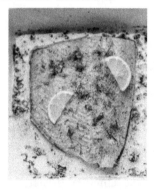

Preparation Time: 10 minutes

Cooking time: 30 minutes

Servings: 4

Ingredients:

1 lb. salmon

1 tablespoon. olive oil

Salt and pepper to taste

1 tablespoon. butter

1 lemon, thinly sliced

1 tablespoon. lemon juice

Directions:

Preheat your oven to 400 degrees F.

Grease a baking dish with the olive oil and place the salmon skin-side down.

Season the salmon with salt and pepper then top with the lemon slices.

Slice half the butter and place over the salmon.

Bake for 20minutes or until the salmon flakes easily. Melt the remaining butter in a saucepan. When it starts to bubble, remove from heat and allow to cool before adding the lemon juice. Drizzle the lemon butter over the salmon and servings warm.

Nutrition:

Calories: 211 kcal Carbs: 1.5 g Fat: 13.5 g

Protein: 22.2 g.

Cauliflower Mash
Preparation Time: 10 minutes

Cooking time: 5 minutes

Servings: 8

Ingredients:

4 cups cauliflower florets, chopped

1 cup grated parmesan cheese

6 tablespoons. butter

½ lemon, juice and zest

Salt and pepper to taste

Directions:

Boil the cauliflower in lightly salted water over high heat for 5 minutes or until the florets are tender but still firm.

Strain the cauliflower in a colander and add the cauliflower to a food processor

Add the remaining ingredients and pulse the mixture to a smooth and creamy consistency

Servings with protein like salmon, chicken or meatballs.

Can be refrigerated for up to 3 days.

Nutrition:

Calories: 101 kcal

Carbs: 3.1 g

Fat: 9.5 g

Protein: 2.2 g.

Baked Salmon

Preparation Time: 10 minutes

Cooking Time: 10 minutes

Servings: 4

Ingredients:

Cooking spray

3 cloves garlic, minced

¼ cup butter

1 teaspoon lemon zest

2 tablespoons lemon juice

4 salmon fillets

Salt and pepper to taste

2 tablespoons parsley, chopped

Directions:

Preheat your oven to 425 degrees F.

Grease the pan with cooking spray.

In a bowl, mix the garlic, butter, lemon zest and lemon juice.

Sprinkle salt and pepper on salmon fillets.

Drizzle with the lemon butter sauce.

Bake in the oven for 12 minutes.

Garnish with parsley before serving.

Nutrition:

Calories 345 - Total Fat 22.7g - Saturated Fat 8.9g

Cholesterol 109mg - Sodium 163mg

Total Carbohydrate 1.2g - Dietary Fiber 0.2g

Total Sugars 0.2g - Protein 34.9g

Potassium 718mg

Tuna Patties

Preparation Time: 10 minutes

Cooking Time: 10 minutes

Servings: 8

Ingredients:

20 oz. canned tuna flakes

¼ cup almond flour

1 egg, beaten

2 tablespoons fresh dill, chopped

2 stalks green onion, chopped

Salt and pepper to taste

1 tablespoon lemon zest

¼ cup mayonnaise

1 tablespoon lemon juice

2 tablespoons avocado oil

Directions:

Combine all the ingredients except avocado oil, lemon juice and avocado oil in a large bowl.

Form 8 patties from the mixture.

In a pan over medium heat, add the oil.

Once the oil starts to sizzle, cook the tuna patties for 3 to 4 minutes per side.

Drain each patty on a paper towel.

Spread mayo on top and drizzle with lemon juice before serving.

Nutrition:

Calories 101 Total Fat 4.9g

Saturated Fat 1.2g Cholesterol 47mg

Sodium 243mg Total Carbohydrate 3.1g

Dietary Fiber 0.5g Total Sugars 0.7g

Protein 12.3g Potassium 60mg

Grilled Mahi Mahi with Lemon Butter Sauce

Preparation Time: 20 minutes

Cooking Time: 10 minutes

Servings: 6

Ingredients:

6 mahi mahi fillets - Salt and pepper to taste

2 tablespoons olive oil - 6 tablespoons butter

¼ onion, minced

½ teaspoon garlic, minced

¼ cup chicken stock

1 tablespoon lemon juice

Directions:

Preheat your grill to medium heat. Season fish fillets with salt and pepper.

Coat both sides with olive oil. Grill for 3 to 4 minutes per side. Place fish on a serving platter. In a pan over medium heat, add the butter and let it melt. Add the onion and sauté for 2 minutes.

Add the garlic and cook for 30 seconds.

Pour in the chicken stock. Simmer until the stock has been reduced to half. Add the lemon juice. Pour the sauce over the grilled fish fillets.

Nutrition:

Calories 234 - Total Fat 17.2g - Saturated Fat 8.3g - Cholesterol 117mg - Sodium 242mg

Total Carbohydrate 0.6g - Dietary Fiber 0.1g - Total Sugars 0.3g - Protein 19.1g –

Potassium 385mg

Shrimp Scampi

Preparation Time: 15 minutes

Cooking Time: 10 minutes

Servings: 6

Ingredients:

2 tablespoons olive oil

2 tablespoons butter

1 tablespoon garlic, minced

½ cup dry white wine

¼ teaspoon red pepper flakes

Salt and pepper to taste

2 lb. large shrimp, peeled and deveined

¼ cup fresh parsley, chopped

1 teaspoon lemon zest

2 tablespoons lemon juice

3 cups spaghetti squash, cooked

Directions:

In a pan over medium heat, add the oil and butter.

Cook the garlic for 2 minutes.

Pour in the wine.

Add the red pepper flakes, salt and pepper.

Cook for 2 minutes.

Add the shrimp.

Cook for 2 to 3 minutes.

Remove from the stove.

Add the parsley, lemon zest and lemon juice.

Serve on top of spaghetti squash.

Nutrition:

Calories 232 Total Fat 8.9g

Saturated Fat 3.2g Cholesterol 226mg

Sodium 229mg Total Carbohydrate 7.6g

Dietary Fiber 0.2g Total Sugars 0.3g

Protein 28.9g Potassium 104mg

Buttered Cod

Preparation Time: 5 minutes

Cooking Time: 5 minutes

Servings: 4

Ingredients: 1 ½ lb. cod fillets, sliced

6 tablespoons butter, sliced

¼ teaspoon garlic powder

¾ teaspoon ground paprika

Salt and pepper to taste

Lemon slices - Chopped parsley

Directions:

Mix the garlic powder, paprika, salt and pepper in a bowl.

Season cod pieces with seasoning mixture.

Add 2 tablespoons butter in a pan over medium heat.

Let half of the butter melt.

Add the cod and cook for 2 minutes per side.

Top with the remaining slices of butter.

Cook for 3 to 4 minutes.

Garnish with parsley and lemon slices before serving.

Nutrition:

Calories 295 - Total Fat 19g - Saturated Fat 11g

Cholesterol 128mg Sodium 236mg - Total Carbohydrate 1.5g

Dietary Fiber 0.7g - Total Sugars 0.3g

Protein 30.7g - Potassium 102mg

Salmon with Red Curry Sauce

Preparation Time: 10 minutes

Cooking Time: 22 minutes

Servings: 4

Ingredients:

4 salmon fillets

2 tablespoons olive oil

Salt and pepper to taste

1 ½ tablespoons red curry paste

1 tablespoon fresh ginger, chopped

14 oz. coconut cream

1 ½ tablespoons fish sauce

Directions:

Preheat your oven to 350 degrees F.

Cover baking sheet with foil.

Brush both sides of salmon fillets with olive oil and season with salt and pepper.

Place the salmon fillets on the baking sheet.

Bake salmon in the oven for 20 minutes.

In a pan over medium heat, mix the curry paste, ginger, coconut cream and fish sauce.

Sprinkle with salt and pepper.

Simmer for 2 minutes.

Pour the sauce over the salmon before serving.

Nutrition:

Calories 553 - Total Fat 43.4g

Saturated Fat 24.1g - Cholesterol 78mg

Sodium 908mg - Total Carbohydrate 7.9g

Dietary Fiber 2.4g - Total Sugars 3.6g - Protein 37.3g - Potassium 982mg

Salmon Teriyaki

Preparation Time: 15 minutes

Cooking Time: 25 minutes

Servings: 6

Ingredients:

3 tablespoons sesame oil

2 teaspoons fish sauce

3 tablespoons coconut amino

2 teaspoons ginger, grated

4 cloves garlic, crushed

2 tablespoons xylitol

1 tablespoon green lime juice

2 teaspoons green lime zest

Cayenne pepper to taste

6 salmon fillets

1 teaspoon arrowroot starch

¼ cup water

Sesame seeds

Directions:

Preheat your oven to 400 degrees F. Combine the sesame oil, fish sauce, coconut amino, ginger, garlic, xylitol, green lime juice, zest and cayenne pepper in a mixing bowl. Create 6 packets using foil. Add half of the marinade in the packets. Add the salmon inside. Place in the baking sheet and cook for about 20 to 25 minutes. Add the remaining sauce in a pan over medium heat. Dissolve arrowroot in water, and add to the sauce. Simmer until the sauce has thickened. Place the salmon on a serving platter and pour the sauce on top. Sprinkle sesame seeds on top before serving.

Nutrition:

Calories 312 Total Fat 17.9g

Saturated Fat 2.6g Cholesterol 78mg

Sodium 242mg Total Carbohydrate 3.5g

Dietary Fiber 0.1g Total Sugars 0.1g

Protein 34.8g

Potassium 706mg

Pesto Shrimp with Zucchini Noodles

Preparation Time: 10 minutes

Cooking Time: 15 minutes

Servings: 3

Ingredients:

Pesto sauce

3 cups basil leaves

¾ cup pine nuts

2 cloves garlic

½ lemon, juiced

1 teaspoon lemon zest

Salt to taste

¼ cup olive oil

Shrimp and Zoodles

3 zucchinis

Salt to taste

1 lb. shrimp

2 tablespoons avocado oil

Directions:

Put all the pesto ingredients in a blender.

Blend until smooth.

Spiralize the zucchini into noodle form.

Season with salt.

Drain water from the zucchini noodles.

Season the shrimp with salt and pepper.

Add half of the oil in a pan over medium heat. Once the oil is hot, add the shrimp and cook for 1 to 2 minutes. Add the remaining oil to the pan.

Add the zucchini noodles and cook for 3 minutes. Add the pesto and toss to coat the noodles evenly with the sauce.

Season with salt.

Nutrition:

Calories 304 Total Fat 22.2g

Saturated Fat 2.6g Cholesterol 159mg

Sodium 223mg Total Carbohydrate 8g

Dietary Fiber 2.3g Total Sugars 2.5g

Protein 21.3g Potassium 547mg

Crab Cakes

Preparation Time: 1 hour and 20 minutes

Cooking Time: 20 minutes

Servings: 8

Ingredients:

2 tablespoons butter

2 cloves garlic, minced

½ cup bell pepper, chopped

1 rib celery, chopped

1 shallot, chopped

Salt and pepper to taste

2 tablespoons mayonnaise

1 egg, beaten

1 teaspoon mustard

1 tablespoon Worcestershire sauce

1 teaspoon hot sauce

½ cup Parmesan cheese, grated

½ cup pork rinds, crushed

1 lb. crabmeat

2 tablespoons olive oil

Directions:

Add the butter to the pan over medium heat.

Add the garlic, bell pepper, celery, shallot, salt and pepper.

Cook for 10 minutes.

In a bowl, mix the mayo, egg, Worcestershire, mustard and hot sauce.

Add the sautéed vegetables to this mixture.

Mix well.

Add the cheese and pork rind.

Fold in the crabmeat.

Line the baking sheet with foil.

Create patties from the mixture.

Place the patties on the baking sheet.

Cover the baking sheet with foil.

Refrigerate for 1 hour.

Fry in olive oil in a pan over medium heat.

Cook until crispy and golden brown.

Nutrition:

Calories 150 Total Fat 9.2g

Saturated Fat 3.2g Cholesterol 43mg

Sodium 601mg

Total Carbohydrate 10.8g Dietary Fiber 0.5g

Total Sugars 4.6g - Protein 6.4g - Potassium 80mg

Tuna Salad

Preparation Time: 5 minutes

Cooking Time: 0 minute

Servings: 2

Ingredients:

1 cup tuna flakes

3 tablespoons mayonnaise

1 teaspoon onion flakes

Salt and pepper to taste

3 cups Romaine lettuce

Directions:

Mix the tuna flakes, mayonnaise, onion flakes, salt and pepper in a bowl.

Serve with lettuce.

Nutrition:

Calories 130 Total Fat 7.8g

Saturated Fat 1.1g Cholesterol 13mg

Sodium 206mg Total Carbohydrate 8.5g

Dietary Fiber 0.6g Total Sugars 2.6g

Protein 8.2g Potassium 132mg

Keto Frosty

Preparation Time: 45 minutes

Cooking Time: 0 minute

Servings: 4

Ingredients:

1 ½ cups heavy whipping cream

2 tablespoons cocoa powder (unsweetened)

3 tablespoons Swerve

1 teaspoon pure vanilla extract

Salt to taste

Directions:

In a bowl, combine all the ingredients. Use a hand mixer and beat until you see stiff peaks forming. Place the mixture in a Ziploc bag. Freeze for 35 minutes. Serve in bowls or dishes.

Nutrition:

Calories 164 Total Fat 17g

Saturated Fat 10.6g Cholesterol 62mg

Sodium 56mg Total Carbohydrate 2.9g

Dietary Fiber 0.8g

Total Sugars 0.2g

Protein 1.4g

Potassium 103mg

Keto Shake

Preparation Time: 15 minutes

Cooking Time: 0 minute

Serving: 1

Ingredients:

¾ cup almond milk

½ cup ice

2 tablespoons almond butter

2 tablespoons cocoa powder (unsweetened)

2 tablespoons Swerve

1 tablespoon chia seeds

2 tablespoons hemp seeds

½ tablespoon vanilla extract

Salt to taste

Directions:

Blend all the ingredients in a food processor.

Chill in the refrigerator before serving.

Nutrition:

Calories 104

Total Fat 9.5g

Saturated Fat 5.1g

Cholesterol 0mg

Sodium 24mg

Total Carbohydrate 3.6g

Dietary Fiber 1.4g

Total Sugars 1.1g

Protein 2.9g - Potassium 159mg

Keto Fat Bombs

Preparation Time: 30 minutes

Cooking Time: 0 minute

Servings: 10

Ingredients:

8 tablespoons butter

¼ cup Swerve

½ teaspoon vanilla extract

Salt to taste

2 cups almond flour

2/3 cup chocolate chips

Directions:

In a bowl, beat the butter until fluffy.

Stir in the sugar, salt and vanilla.

Mix well.

Add the almond flour.

Fold in the chocolate chips.

Cover the bowl with cling wrap and refrigerate for 20 minutes.

Create balls from the dough.

Nutrition:

Calories 176

Total Fat 15.2g Saturated Fat 8.4g

Cholesterol 27mg Sodium 92mg

Total Carbohydrate 12.9g

Dietary Fiber 1g - Total Sugars 10.8g

Protein 2.2g - Potassium 45mg

Avocado Ice Pops

Preparation Time: 20 minutes

Cooking Time: 0 minute

Servings: 10

Ingredients:

3 avocados

¼ cup lime juice

3 tablespoons Swerve

¾ cup coconut milk

1 tablespoon coconut oil

1 cup keto friendly chocolate

Directions:

Add all the ingredients except the oil and chocolate in a blender.

Blend until smooth.

Pour the mixture into the popsicle mold.

Freeze overnight.

In a bowl, mix oil and chocolate chips.

Melt in the microwave. And then let cool.

Dunk the avocado popsicles into the chocolate before serving.

Nutrition:

Calories 176 Total Fat 17.4g

Saturated Fat 7.5g Cholesterol 0mg

Sodium 6mg - Total Carbohydrate 10.8g

Dietary Fiber 4.5g - Total Sugars 5.4g

Protein 1.6g - Potassium 341mg

Carrot Balls

Preparation Time: 1 hour and 10 minutes

Cooking Time: 0 minute

Servings: 8

Ingredients:

8 oz. block cream cheese

¾ cup coconut flour

½ teaspoon pure vanilla extract

1 teaspoon stevia

¼ teaspoon ground nutmeg

1 teaspoon cinnamon

1 cup carrots, grated

1/2 cup pecans, chopped

1 cup coconut, shredded

Directions:

Use a hand mixer to beat the cream cheese, coconut flour, vanilla, stevia, nutmeg and cinnamon.

Fold in the carrots and pecans.

Form into balls.

Refrigerate for 1 hour.

Roll into shredded coconut before serving.

Nutrition:

Calories 390 Total Fat 35g

Saturated Fat 17g Cholesterol 60mg

Sodium 202mg Total Carbohydrate 17.2g

Dietary Fiber 7.8g Total Sugars 6g

Protein 7.8g Potassium 154mg

Coconut Crack Bars

Preparation Time: 2 minutes

Cooking Time: 3 minutes

Servings: 20

Ingredients:

3 cups coconut flakes (unsweetened)

1 cup coconut oil

¼ cup maple syrup

Directions:

Line a baking sheet with parchment paper.

Put coconut in a bowl.

Add the oil and syrup.

Mix well.

Pour the mixture into the pan.

Refrigerate until firm.

Slice into bars before serving.

Nutrition:

Calories 147

Total Fat 14.9g

Saturated Fat 13g

Cholesterol 0mg

Sodium 3mg

Total Carbohydrate 4.5g

Dietary Fiber 1.1g

Total Sugars 3.1g

Protein 0.4g

Potassium 51mg

Strawberry Ice Cream

Preparation Time: 1 hour and 20 minutes

Cooking Time: 0 minute

Servings: 4

Ingredients:

17 oz. coconut milk

16 oz. frozen strawberries

¾ cup Swerve

½ cup fresh strawberries

Directions:

Put all the ingredients except fresh strawberries in a blender.

Pulse until smooth.

Put the mixture in an ice cream maker.

Use ice cream maker according to directions.

Add the fresh strawberries a few minutes before the ice cream is done.

Freeze for 1 hour before serving.

Nutrition:

Calories 320

Total Fat 28.8g

Saturated Fat 25.5g

Cholesterol 0mg Sodium 18mg

Total Carbohydrate 25.3g

Dietary Fiber 5.3g Total Sugars 19.1g

Protein 2.9g

Potassium 344mg

Key Lime Pudding

Preparation Time: 20 minutes

Cooking Time: 1 hour and 15 minutes

Servings: 2

Ingredients:

1 cup hot water

2/4 cup erythrytol syrup

6 drops stevia

1 teaspoon almond extract

1 teaspoon vanilla extract

¼ teaspoon Xanthan gum powder

2 ripe avocados, sliced

1 ½ oz. lime juice

3 tablespoons coconut oil

Salt to taste

Directions:

Add water, erythritol, stevia, almond extract and vanilla extract to a pot.

Bring to a boil.

Simmer until the syrup has been reduced and has thickened.

Turn the heat off.

Add the gum powder.

Mix until thickened.

Add the avocado into a food processor.

Add the rest of the ingredients.

Pulse until smooth.

Place the mixture in ramekins.

Refrigerate for 1 hour.

Pour the syrup over the pudding before serving.

Nutrition:

Calories 299

Total Fat 29.8g

Saturated Fat 12.9g

Cholesterol 0mg

Sodium 47mg

Total Carbohydrate 9.7g

Dietary Fiber 6.8g

Total Sugars 0.8g

Protein 2g

Potassium 502mg

Chicken in Sweet and Sour Sauce with Corn Salad

Preparation Time: 10 minutes

Cooking time: 15 minutes

Servings: 4

Ingredients:

2 cups plus 2 tablespoons of unflavored low-fat yoghurt

2 cups of frozen mango chunks

3 tablespoons of honey

¼ cup plus 1 tablespoon apple cider vinegar

¼ cup sultana

2 tablespoons of olive oil, plus an amount to be brushed

¼ teaspoon of cayenne pepper

5 dried tomatoes (not in oil)

2 small cloves of garlic, finely chopped

4 cobs, peeled

8 peeled and boned chicken legs, peeled (about 700g)

Halls

6 cups of mixed salad

2 medium carrots, finely sliced

Directions:

For the smoothie: in a blender, mix 2 cups of yogurt, 2 cups of ice, 1 cup of mango and all the honey until the mixture becomes completely smooth. Divide into 4 glasses and refrigerate until ready to use. Rinse the blender.

Preheat the grill to medium-high heat. Mix the remaining cup of mango, ¼ cup water, ¼ cup vinegar, sultanas, olive oil, cayenne pepper, tomatoes and garlic in a microwave bowl. Cover with a piece of clear film and cook in the microwave until the tomatoes become soft, for about 3 minutes. Leave to cool slightly and pass in a blender. Transfer to a small bowl. Leave 2 tablespoons aside to garnish, turn the chicken into the remaining mixture.

Put the corn on the grill, cover and bake, turning it over if necessary, until it is burnt, about 10 minutes. Remove and keep warm.

Brush the grill over medium heat and brush the grills with a little oil. Turn the chicken legs into half the remaining sauce and ½ teaspoon of salt. Put on the grill and cook until the cooking marks appear and the

internal temperature reaches 75°C on an instantaneous thermometer, 8 to 10 minutes per side. Bart and sprinkle a few times with the remaining sauce while cooking.

While the chicken is cooking, beat the remaining 2 tablespoons of yogurt, the 2 tablespoons of sauce set aside, the remaining spoonful of vinegar, 1 tablespoon of water and ¼ teaspoon of salt in a large bowl. Mix the mixed salad with the carrots. Divide chicken, corn and salad into 4 serving dishes. Garnish the salad with the dressing set aside. Serve each plate with a mango smoothie.

Nutrition:

Calories 346

Protein 56

Fat 45

Chinese Chicken Salad

Preparation Time: 15 minutes

Cooking time: 30 minutes

Servings: 4

Ingredients:

For the chicken salad:

4 divided chicken breasts with skin and bones

Olive oil of excellent quality

Salt and freshly ground black pepper

500 g asparagus, with the ends removed and cut into three parts diagonally

1 red pepper, peeled

Chinese condiment, recipe to follow

2 spring onions (both the white and the green part), sliced diagonally

1 tablespoon of white sesame seeds, toasted

For Chinese dressing:

120 ml vegetable oil

60 ml of apple cider vinegar of excellent quality

60 ml soy sauce

1 ½ tablespoon of black sesame

½ tablespoon of honey

1 clove of garlic, minced

½ teaspoon of fresh peeled and grated ginger

½ tablespoon sesame seeds, toasted

60 g peanut butter

2 teaspoons of salt

½ teaspoons freshly ground black pepper

Directions:

For the chicken salad:

Heat the oven to 180°C (or 200°C for gas oven). Put the chicken breast on a baking tray and rub the skin with a little olive oil. Season freely with salt and pepper.

Brown for 35 to 40 minutes, until the chicken is freshly cooked. Let it cool down as long as it takes to handle it. Remove the meat from the bones, remove the skin and chop the chicken into medium-sized pieces.

Blanch the asparagus in a pot of salted water for 3-5 minutes until tender. Soak them in water with ice to stop cooking. Drain them. Cut the peppers into strips the same size as the asparagus. In a large bowl, mix the chopped chicken, asparagus and peppers.

Spread the Chinese dressing on chicken and vegetables. Add the spring onions and sesame seeds, and season to taste. Serve cold or at room temperature.

For Chinese dressing:

Mix all ingredients and set aside until use.

Nutrition:

Calories 222 Protein 28

Fat 10 Sugar 6

Chicken Salad
Preparation Time: 15 minutes

Cooking time: 25 minutes

Servings: 4

Ingredients:

For the Buffalo chicken salad:

2 chicken breasts (225 g) peeled, boned, cut in half

2 tablespoons of hot cayenne pepper sauce (or another type of hot sauce), plus an addition depending on taste

2 tablespoons of olive oil

2 romaine lettuce heart, cut into 2 cm strips

4 celery stalks, finely sliced

2 carrots, roughly grated

2 fresh onions, only the green part, sliced

125 ml of blue cheese dressing, recipe to follow

For the seasoning of blue cheese

2 tablespoons mayonnaise

70 ml of partially skimmed buttermilk

70 ml low-fat white yoghurt

1 tablespoon of wine vinegar

½ teaspoon of sugar

35 g of chopped blue cheese

Salt and freshly ground black pepper

Directions:

For the Buffalo chicken salad:

Preheat the grid.

Place the chicken between 2 sheets of baking paper and beat it with a meat tenderizer so that it is about 2 cm thick, then cut the chicken sideways creating 1 cm strips.

In a large bowl, add the hot sauce and oil, add the chicken and turn it over until it is well soaked. Place the chicken on a baking tray and grill until well cooked, about 4-6 minutes, turning it once.

In a large bowl, add the lettuce, celery, grated carrots and fresh onions. Add the seasoning of blue cheese. Distribute the vegetables in 4 plates and arrange the chicken on each of the dishes. Serve with hot sauce on the side.

For the blue cheese dressing:

Cover a small bowl with absorbent paper folded in four. Spread the yoghurt on the paper and put it in the fridge for 20 minutes to drain and firm it.

In a medium bowl, beat the buttermilk and firm yogurt with mayonnaise until well blended. Add the vinegar and sugar and keep beating until well blended. Add the blue cheese and season with salt and pepper to taste.

Nutrition:

321 calories

Fat 3 Fiber 5

Carbs 7 Protein 4

Tofu Meat and Salad
Preparation Time: 15 minutes

Cooking time: 20 minutes

Servings: 3

Ingredients:

1 tablespoon of garlic sauce and chili in a bottle

1 1/2 tablespoon sesame oil

3 tablespoons of low-sodium soy sauce

60 ml hoisin sauce

2 tablespoons rice vinegar

2 tablespoons of sherry or Chinese cooking wine

225 g of extra-solid tofu

2 teaspoons of rapeseed oil

2 tablespoons of finely chopped fresh ginger

4 spring onions, with the green part chopped and set aside, in thin slices

225 g of minced lean beef (90% or more lean)

25 g of diced Chinese water chestnuts

1 large head of cappuccino lettuce, with the leaves separated, but without the outer ones

1 red pepper, diced

Directions:

In a bowl, mix together the garlic and chili sauce, sesame oil, soy sauce, hoisin sauce, vinegar and sherry. Cut the tofu into 1 cm thick slices and place them on a kitchen towel. Use the cloth to dab the tofu well to remove as much water as possible. Should take a couple of minutes and about three dish towels. Chop the dry tofu well and set aside. Heat the oil in a wok or in a very large pan and medium flame. Add the ginger and the white part of the spring onions and cook until the spring onions become translucent and the ginger fragrant, for about 2-3 minutes. Add the beef and tofu and cook, stirring, until the meat becomes dull and freshly cooked, for about 4-5 minutes. Add the sauce set aside. Reduce the flame and simmer slowly, stirring, for another 3-4 minutes. Add the chestnuts and mix well to incorporate. Fill each lettuce leaf with stuffing. Serve by decorating with the green part of the spring onions, red pepper and peanuts.

Nutrition:

Calories 122 Fat 2 Protein 66

Asparagus and Pistachios Vinaigrette

Preparation Time: 10 minutes

Cooking time: 5minutes

Servings: 2

Ingredients:

Two 455g bunches of large asparagus, without the tip

1 tablespoon of olive oil

Salt and freshly ground black pepper

6 tablespoons of sliced pistachios blanched and boiled

1 1/2 tablespoon lemon juice

1/4 teaspoon of sugar

1 1/2 teaspoon lemon zest

Directions:

Preheat the oven to 220°C. Put the grill in the top third of the oven. Place the asparagus on a baking tray covered with baking paper. Sprinkle with olive oil and season with a little salt and pepper. Bake for 15 minutes, until soft.

Meanwhile, blend 5 tablespoons of almonds, lemon juice, sugar and 6 tablespoons of water for 1 minute until smooth. Taste and regulate salt. Pour the sauce on a plate and put the spinach on the sauce. Decorate with peel and the remaining spoon of pistachios

Nutrition:

Calories 560

Fat 5 Fiber 2

Carbs 3 Protein 9

Turkey Meatballs

Preparation Time: 30 minutes

Cooking time: 0 minutes

Servings: 4

Ingredients:

255g turkey sausage

2 tablespoons of extra virgin olive oil

One can of 425g chickpeas, rinsed and drained...

1/2 medium onion, chopped, 2/3 cup

2 cloves of garlic, finely chopped

1 teaspoon of cumin

1/2 cup flour

1/2 teaspoon instant yeast for desserts

Salt and ground black pepper

1 cup of Greek yogurt

2 tablespoons of lime juice

2 radicchio hearts, chopped

Hot sauce

Directions:

Preheat the oven to 200°C.

In a processor, blend the chickpeas, onion, garlic, cumin, 1 teaspoon salt and 1/2 teaspoon pepper until all the ingredients are finely chopped. Add the flour, baking powder and blend to make everything mix well. Transfer to a medium bowl and add the sausage, stirring together with your hands. Cover and refrigerate for 30 minutes.

Once cold, take the mixture in spoonful, forming 1-inch balls with wet hands. Heat the olive oil in a pan over medium heat. In two groups, put the falafel in the pan and cook until slightly brown, about a minute and a half per side. Transfer to a baking tray and bake in the oven until well cooked, for about 10 minutes.

Mix together the yogurt, lime juice, 1/2 teaspoon salt and 1/4 teaspoon pepper. Divide the lettuce into 4 plates, season with some yogurt sauce.

Nutrition:

Calories 189

Fat 5

Protein 77

Sugar 3

Trout and Chili Nuts

Preparation Time: 10 minutes

Cooking time: 0 minutes

Servings: 3

Ingredients:

1.5kg of rainbow trout

300gr shelled walnuts

1 bunch of parsley

9 cloves of garlic

7 tablespoons of olive oil

2 fresh hot peppers

The juice of 2 lemons

Halls

Directions:

Clean and dry the trout then place them in a baking tray.

Chop the walnuts, parsley and chili peppers then mash the garlic cloves.

Mix the ingredients by adding olive oil, lemon juice and a pinch of salt.

Stuff the trout with some of the sauce and use the rest to cover the fish.

Bake at 180° for 30/40 minutes.

Serve the trout hot or cold.

Nutrition:

Calories 226

Fat 5

Fiber 2

Carbs 7

Protein 8

Nut Granola & Smoothie Bowl

Preparation Time: 10 minutes

Cooking time: 40 minutes

Servings: 3

Ingredients:

6 cups Greek yogurt

4 tablespoon almond butter

A handful toasted walnuts

3 tablespoon unsweetened cocoa powder

4 teaspoon swerve brown sugar

2 cups nut granola for topping

Directions:

Combine the Greek yogurt, almond butter, walnuts, cocoa powder, and swerve brown sugar in a smoothie maker; puree in high-speed until smooth and well mixed.

Share the smoothie into four breakfast bowls, top with a half cup of granola each, and serve.

Nutrition:

Kcal 361,

Fat 31.2g,

Net Carbs 2g,

Protein 13g

Bacon and Egg Quesadillas

Preparation Time: 10 minutes

Cooking time: 30 minutes

Servings: 3

Ingredients:

8 low carb tortilla shells

6 eggs

1 cup water

3 tablespoon butter

1 ½ cups grated cheddar cheese

1 ½ cups grated Swiss cheese

5 bacon slices

1 medium onion, thinly sliced

1 tablespoon chopped parsley

Directions

Bring the eggs to a boil in water over medium heat for 10 minutes. Transfer the eggs to an ice water bath, peel the shells, and chop them; set aside.

Meanwhile, as the eggs cook, fry the bacon in a skillet over medium heat for 4 minutes until crispy. Remove and chop. Plate and set aside too.

Fetch out 2/3 of the bacon fat and sauté the onions in the remaining grease over medium heat for 2 minutes; set aside. Melt 1 tablespoon of butter in a skillet over medium heat.Lay one tortilla in a skillet; sprinkle with some Swiss cheese. Add some chopped eggs and bacon over the cheese, top with onion, and sprinkle with some cheddar cheese. Cover with another tortilla shell. Cook for 45 seconds, then carefully flip the quesadilla, and cook the other side too for 45 seconds. Remove to a plate and repeat the cooking process using the remaining tortilla shells.

Garnish with parsley and serve warm.

Nutrition:

Kcal 449, Fat 48.7g, Net Carbs 6.8g,

Protein 29.1g

Avocado and Kale Eggs
Preparation Time: 10 minutes

Cooking time: 30 minutes

Servings: 3

Ingredients:

1 teaspoon ghee

1 red onion, sliced

4 oz chorizo, sliced into thin rounds

1 cup chopped kale

1 ripe avocado, pitted, peeled, chopped

4 eggs

Salt and black pepper to season

Directions:

Preheat oven to 370ºF.

Melt ghee in a cast iron pan over medium heat and sauté the onion for 2 minutes. Add the chorizo and cook for 2 minutes more, flipping once. Introduce the kale in batches with a splash of water to wilt, season lightly with salt, stir and cook for 3 minutes. Mix in the avocado and turn the heat off. Create four holes in the mixture, crack the eggs into each hole, sprinkle with salt and black pepper, and slide the pan into the preheated oven to bake for 6 minutes until the egg whites are set or firm and yolks still runny. Season to taste with salt and pepper, and serve right away with low carb toasts.

Nutrition:

Kcal 274, Fat 23g, Net Carbs 4g,

Protein 13g

Bacon and Cheese Frittata
Preparation Time: 10 minutes

Cooking time: 20 minutes

Servings: 3

Ingredients:

10 slices bacon

10 fresh eggs

3 tablespoon butter, melted

½ cup almond milk

Salt and black pepper to taste

1 ½ cups cheddar cheese, shredded

¼ cup chopped green onions

Directions:

Preheat the oven to 400°F and grease a baking dish with cooking spray. Cook the bacon in a skillet over medium heat for 6 minutes. Once crispy, remove from the skillet to paper towels and discard grease. Chop into small pieces. Whisk the eggs, butter, milk, salt, and black pepper. Mix in the bacon and pour the mixture into the baking dish. Sprinkle with cheddar cheese and green onions, and bake in the oven for 10 minutes or until the eggs are thoroughly cooked. Remove and cool the frittata for 3 minutes, slice into wedges, and serve warm with a dollop of Greek yogurt.

Nutrition:

Kcal 325, Fat 28g,

Net Carbs 2g, Protein 15g

Spicy Egg Muffins with Bacon & heese

Preparation Time: 10 minutes

Cooking time: 20 minutes

Servings: 3

Ingredients:

12 eggs

¼ cup coconut milk

Salt and black pepper to taste

1 cup grated cheddar cheese

12 slices bacon

4 jalapeño peppers, seeded and minced

Directions:

Preheat oven to 370°F.

Crack the eggs into a bowl and whisk with coconut milk until combined. Season with salt and pepper, and evenly stir in the cheddar cheese. Line each hole of a muffin tin with a slice of bacon and fill each with the egg mixture two-thirds way up. Top with the jalapeno peppers and bake in the oven for 18 to 20 minutes or until puffed and golden. Remove, allow cooling for a few minutes, and serve with arugula salad.

Nutrition:

Kcal 302, Fat 23.7g, Net Carbs 3.2g,

Protein 20g

Ham & Egg Broccoli Bake

Preparation Time: 10 minutes

Cooking time: 25 minutes

Servings: 3

Ingredients:

2 heads broccoli, cut into small florets

2 red bell peppers, seeded and chopped

¼ cup chopped ham

2 teaspoon ghee

1 teaspoon dried oregano + extra to garnish

Salt and black pepper to taste

8 fresh eggs

Directions

Preheat oven to 425°F.

Melt the ghee in a frying pan over medium heat; brown the ham, stirring frequently, about 3 minutes.

Arrange the broccoli, bell peppers, and ham on a foil-lined baking sheet in a single layer, toss to combine; season with salt, oregano, and black pepper. Bake for 10 minutes until the vegetables have softened.

Remove, create eight indentations with a spoon, and crack an egg into each. Return to the oven and continue to bake for an additional 5 to 7 minutes until the egg whites are firm.

Season with salt, black pepper, and extra oregano, share the bake into four plates and serve with strawberry lemonade (optional).

Nutrition:

Kcal 344, Fat 28g, Net Carbs 4.2g,

Protein 11g

Italian Sausage Stacks
Preparation Time: 10 minutes

Cooking time: 25 minutes

Servings: 3

Ingredients:

6 Italian sausage patties

4 tablespoon olive oil

2 ripe avocados, pitted

2 teaspoon fresh lime juice

Salt and black pepper to taste

6 fresh eggs

Red pepper flakes to garnish

Directions:

In a skillet, warm the oil over medium heat and fry the sausage patties about 8 minutes until lightly browned and firm. Remove the patties to a plate. Spoon the avocado into a bowl, mash with the lime juice, and season with salt and black pepper. Spread the mash on the sausages. Boil 3 cups of water in a wide pan over high heat, and reduce to simmer (don't boil). Crack each egg into a small bowl and gently put the egg into the simmering water; poach for 2 to 3 minutes. Use a perforated spoon to remove from the water on a paper towel to dry. Repeat with the other 5 eggs. Top each stack with a poached egg, sprinkle with chili flakes, salt, black pepper, and chives. Serve with turnip wedges.

Nutrition:

Kcal 378, Fat 23g, Net Carbs 5g,

Protein 16g

Dark Chocolate Smoothie
Preparation Time: 10 minutes

Cooking time: 25 minutes

Servings: 3

Ingredients:

8 pecans

¾ cup coconut milk

¼ cup water

1 ½ cups watercress

2 teaspoon vegan protein powder

1 tablespoon chia seeds

1 tablespoon unsweetened cocoa powder

4 fresh dates, pitted

Directions

In a blender, add all ingredients and process until creamy and uniform. Place into two glasses and chill before serving.

Nutrition:

Kcal 335;

Fat: 31.7g

Net Carbs: 12.7g,

Protein: 7g

Five Greens Smoothie

Preparation Time: 10 minutes

Cooking time: 25 minutes

Servings: 3

Ingredients:

6 kale leaves, chopped

3 stalks celery, chopped

1 ripe avocado, skinned, pitted, sliced

1 cup ice cubes

2 cups spinach, chopped

1 large cucumber, peeled and chopped

Chia seeds to garnish

Directions:

In a blender, add the kale, celery, avocado, and ice cubes, and blend for 45 seconds. Add the spinach and cucumber, and process for another 45 seconds until smooth.

Pour the smoothie into glasses, garnish with chia seeds and serve the drink immediately.

Nutrition:

Kcal 124,

Fat 7.8g,

Net Carbs 2.9g,

Protein 3.2g

Almond Waffles with Cinnamon Cream

Preparation Time: 10 minutes

Cooking time: 25 minutes

Servings: 3

Ingredients:

For the Spread

8 oz cream cheese, at room temperature

1 teaspoon cinnamon powder

3 tablespoon swerve brown sugar

Cinnamon powder for garnishing

For the Waffles

5 tablespoon melted butter

1 ½ cups unsweetened almond milk

7 large eggs

¼ teaspoon liquid stevia

½ teaspoon baking powder

1 ½ cups almond flour

Directions:

Combine the cream cheese, cinnamon, and swerve with a hand mixer until smooth. Cover and chill until ready to use. To make the waffles, whisk the butter, milk, and eggs in a medium bowl. Add the stevia and baking powder and mix. Stir in the almond flour and combine until no lumps exist. Let the batter sit for 5 minutes to thicken. Spritz a waffle iron with a non-stick cooking spray. Ladle a ¼ cup of the batter into the waffle iron and cook according to the manufacturer's instructions until golden, about 10 minutes in total. Repeat with the remaining batter. Slice the waffles into quarters; apply the cinnamon spread in between each of two waffles and snap. Sprinkle with cinnamon powder and serve.

Nutrition:

Kcal 307, Fat 24g, Net Carbs 8g, Protein 12g

Smoked Salmon Rolls with Dill Cream Cheese

Preparation Time: 10 minutes

Cooking time: 25 minutes

Servings: 3

Ingredients:

3 tablespoon cream cheese, softened

1 small lemon, zested and juiced

3 teaspoon chopped fresh dill

Salt and black pepper to taste

3 (7-inch) low carb tortillas

6 slices smoked salmon

Directions

In a bowl, mix the cream cheese, lemon juice, zest, dill, salt, and black pepper.

Lay each tortilla on a plastic wrap (just wide enough to cover the tortilla), spread with cream cheese mixture, and top each (one) with two salmon slices. Roll up the tortillas and secure both ends by twisting.

Refrigerate for 2 hours, remove plastic, cut off both ends of each wrap, and cut wraps into wheels.

Nutrition:

Kcal 250,

Fat 16g,

Net Carbs 7g,

Protein 18g

CHAPTER 11: Dinner Recipes

Pork Chops with Bacon & Mushrooms

Preparation Time: 10 minutes

Cooking Time: 20 minutes

Servings: 4

Ingredients:

6 strips bacon, chopped

4 pork chops

Salt and pepper to taste

2 cloves garlic, minced

8 oz. mushrooms, sliced

1 tablespoon olive oil

5 sprigs fresh thyme

2/3 cup chicken broth

1/2 cup heavy cream

Directions:

Cook bacon in a pan until crispy. Transfer bacon on a plate. Sprinkle salt and pepper on the pork chops. Cook the pork chops in bacon fat for 4 minutes per side. Transfer pork chops on a plate. Add the garlic and mushrooms in the pan. Add the olive oil Cook for 5 minutes. Pour in the broth and let the mixture boil. Stir in the heavy cream and reduce the heat to low. Put the bacon and pork chops back to the pan.

Cook for 3 more minutes before serving.

Nutrition:

Calories 516

Total Fat 41.3g

Saturated Fat 15.4g

Cholesterol 121mg

Sodium 851mg

Total Carbohydrate 4.2g

Dietary Fiber 1.1g

Total Sugars 1.2g

Protein 31.7g

Potassium 679mg

Pork

Preparation Time: 10 minutes

Cooking Time: 20 minutes

Servings: 4

Ingredients:

A single pound of pork tenderloin

A quarter cup of oil

3 medium shallots (chop them finely)

Directions:

Slice your pork into thick slices (go for about a half-inch thick).

Chop up your shallots before placing them on a plate.

Get a cast-iron skillet and warm up the oil

Press your pork into your shallots on both sides. Press firmly to make sure that they stick.

Place the slices of pork with shallots into the warm oil and then cook until it's done. The shallots may burn, but they will still be fine.

Make sure the pork is cooked through thoroughly.

Nutrition:

Calories-519

Fat-36 grams

Protein-46 grams

Carbs-7 grams

Garlic Shrimp

Preparation Time: 10 minutes

Cooking Time: 30 minutes

Servings: 4

Ingredients:

2 minced garlic cloves

2 whole garlic cloves

The juice from half a lemon

2 tablespoons of oil (olive)

2 tablespoons of butter

¾ pounds of either small or medium shrimp (it needs to be both shelled and deveined)

A quarter of a teaspoon of paprika

A quarter of a teaspoon of pepper flakes (red ones)

2 tablespoons of parsley that is chopped.

Directions:

Sprinkle your shrimp with a teaspoon of salt (fine grain sea salt) and let it sit for ten minutes.

Get a skillet.

Heat the butter with olive oil over a heat that is medium-high.

Add the flakes and garlic.

Sauté for half a minute.

Add your shrimp and cook until they have turned pink. This will take approximately two minutes. Stir constantly.

Add paprika and juice from the lemon.

Cook for another sixty seconds.

Nutrition

Per serving

Calories-260 - Fat-18 grams - Carbs-none - Protein-24 protein

Pork Chop

Preparation Time: 10 minutes

Cooking Time: 30 minutes

Servings: 2

Ingredients:

A dozen pork chop (boneless and thin cut)

2 cups of spinach (you should use baby spinach for this)

4 cloves of garlic

A dozen slices provolone cheese

Directions:

Preheat your oven to a temperature of 350.

Press the garlic cloves using a garlic press. The cloves should go through the press and into a small bowl. Spread the garlic that you have made onto one side of the pork chops. Flip half a dozen chops while making sure the garlic side is down. You should do this on a baking sheet that is rimmed. Divide your spinach between the half dozen chops. Fold cheese slices in half. Put them on top of the spinach.

Put a second pork chop on top of the first set, but this time make sure that the garlic side is up. Bake for 20 minutes. Cover each chop with another piece of cheese. Bake another 15 minutes.

Your meat meter should be at 160 degrees when you check with a thermometer.

Nutrition:

Calories-436 - Fat-25 grams - Carbs-2 grams

Protein-47 grams

Citrus Egg Salad
Preparation Time: 10 minutes

Cooking Time: 20 minutes

Servings: 3

Ingredients:

Half a dozen eggs (6)

A single teaspoon of mustard (go with Dijon)

2 tablespoons of mayo

A single teaspoon of lemon juice

Directions:

Place the eggs gently in a medium saucepan.

Add cold water until your eggs are covered by an inch.

Bring to a boil.

You should do this for ten minutes. Remove from your heat and cool. Peel your eggs under running water that is cold.

Put your eggs in a food processor. Pulse until they are chopped.

Stir in condiments and juice.

Nutrition:

Calories-222

Fat-19 grams

Protein-13 grams

Carbs-1 gram

Chowder
Preparation Time: 10 minutes

Cooking Time: 30 minutes

Servings: 4

Ingredients:

A single tablespoon of butter

5 minced garlic cloves

An entire head of cauliflower (cut it into florets that are small)

Half of a teaspoon of oregano (use dried) - Half a cup of carrots that have been diced

Half a cup of onions that have been diced

A cup and a half of broth (use vegetable)

A quarter cup of cream cheese

Directions:

Get a soup pot. Heat your butter.

Add garlic and onions. Sauté for a few moments.

Add the rest of the ingredients to the pot.

Bring to a boil. Slow the heat and put it on a simmer.

Cook for 15 minutes. Shut off the flame. Use a hand blender to blend the soup partly in the pot.

Switch the flame back on.

Add a cup of broth.

Add the cream cheese.

Simmer for 10 minutes and switch off the flame again.

Nutrition:

Calories-143 Fat-8.4 grams

Carbs-15.2 grams Protein-4.5 grams

Bulgur Appetizer Salad

Preparation Time: 30 minutes

Cooking time: 0 minutes

Servings: 4

Ingredients:

1 cup bulgur

2 cups hot water

Black pepper to the taste

2 cups corn

1 cucumber, chopped

2 tablespoons lemon juice

2 tablespoons balsamic vinegar

¼ cup olive oil

Directions:

In a bowl, mix bulgur with the water, cover, leave aside for 30 minutes, fluff with a fork and transfer to a salad bowl. Add corn, cucumber, oil with lemon juice, vinegar and pepper, toss, divide into small cups and serve.

Nutrition:

Calories 130 Fat 2

Fiber 2 Carbs 7 Protein 6

Cocoa Bars

Preparation Time: 2 hours

Cooking time: 0 minutes

Servings: 12

Ingredients:

1 cup unsweetened cocoa chips

2 cups rolled oats

1 cup low-fat peanut butter

½ cup chia seeds

½ cup raisins

¼ cup coconut sugar

½ cup coconut milk

Directions:

Put 1 and ½ cups oats in your blender, pulse well, transfer this to a bowl, add the rest of the oats, cocoa chips, chia seeds, raisins, sugar and milk, stir really well, spread this into a square pan, press well, keep in the fridge for 2 hours, slice into 12 bars and serve.

Nutrition:

Calories 198 Fat 5

Fiber 4 Carbs 10 Protein 89

Cinnamon Apple Chips

Preparation Time: 10 minutes

Cooking time: 2 hours

Servings: 4

Ingredients:

Cooking spray

2 teaspoons cinnamon powder

2 apples, cored and thinly sliced

Directions:

Arrange apple slices on a lined baking sheet, spray them with cooking oil, sprinkle cinnamon, introduce in the oven and bake at 300 degrees F for 2 hours. ivide into bowls and serve as a snack.

Nutrition:

Calories 80

Fat 0 Fiber 3

Carbs 7 Protein 4

Greek Party Dip

Preparation Time: 10 minutes

Cooking time: 0 minutes

Servings: 4

Ingredients:

½ cup coconut cream

1 cup fat-free Greek yogurt

2 teaspoons dill, dried

2 teaspoons thyme, dried

1 teaspoon sweet paprika

2 teaspoons no-salt-added sun-dried tomatoes, chopped

2 teaspoons parsley, chopped

2 teaspoons chives, chopped

Black pepper to the taste

Directions:

In a bowl, mix cream with yogurt, dill with thyme, paprika, tomatoes, parsley, chives and pepper, stir well, divide into smaller bowls and serve as a dip.

Nutrition:

Calories 100

Fat 1

Fiber 4

Carbs 8

Protein 3

Spicy Pumpkin Seeds Bowls

Preparation Time: 10 minutes

Cooking time: 20 minutes

Servings: 6

Ingredients: ½ tablespoon chili powder

½ teaspoon cayenne pepper

2 cups pumpkin seeds - 2 teaspoons lime juice

Directions:

Spread pumpkin seeds on a lined baking sheet, add lime juice, cayenne and chili powder, toss well, introduce in the oven, roast at 275 degrees F for 20 minutes, divide into small bowls and serve as a snack.

Nutrition:

Calories 170 Fat 2 Fiber 7

Carbs 12 Protein 6

Apple and Pecans Bowls

Preparation Time: 10 minutes

Cooking time: 0 minutes

Servings: 4

Ingredients:

4 big apples, cored, peeled and cubed

2 teaspoons lemon juice

¼ cup pecans, chopped

Directions:

In a bowl, mix apples with lemon juice and pecans, toss, divide into small bowls and serve as a snack.

Nutrition:

Calories 120 Fat 4

Fiber 3 Carbs 12 Protein 3

Shrimp Muffins

Preparation Time: 10 minutes

Cooking time: 45 minutes

Servings: 6

Ingredients:

1 spaghetti squash, peeled and halved

2 tablespoons avocado mayonnaise

1 cup low-fat mozzarella cheese, shredded

8 ounces' shrimp, peeled, cooked and chopped

1 and ½ cups almond flour

1 teaspoon parsley, dried

1 garlic clove, minced

Black pepper to the taste

Cooking spray

Directions:

Arrange the squash on a lined baking sheet, introduce in the oven at 375 degrees F, bake for 30 minutes, scrape flesh into a bowl, add pepper, parsley flakes, flour, shrimp, mayo and mozzarella and stir well, divide this mix into a muffin tray greased with cooking spray, bake in the oven at 375 degrees F for 15 minutes and serve them cold as a snack.

Nutrition:

Calories 140 Fat 2 Fiber 4

Carbs 14 Protein 12

Zucchini Bowls

Preparation Time: 10 minutes

Cooking time: 20 minutes

Servings: 12

Ingredients:

Cooking spray - ½ cup dill, chopped

1 egg - ½ cup whole wheat flour

Black pepper to the taste

1 yellow onion, chopped

2 garlic cloves, minced

3 zucchinis, grated

Directions:

In a bowl, mix zucchinis with garlic, onion, flour, pepper, egg and dill, stir well, shape small bowls out of this mix, arrange them on a lined baking sheet, grease them with some cooking spray, bake at 400 degrees F for 20 minutes, flipping them halfway, divide them into bowls and serve as a snack.

Nutrition:

Calories 120, Fat 1

Fiber 4 Carbs 12 Protein 6

Cheesy Mushrooms Caps

Preparation Time: 10 minutes

Cooking time: 30 minutes

Servings: 20

Ingredients: 20 white mushroom caps

1 garlic clove, minced

3 tablespoons parsley, chopped

2 yellow onions, chopped

Black pepper to the taste

½ cup low-fat parmesan, grated

¼ cup low-fat mozzarella, grated

A drizzle of olive oil

2 tablespoons non-fat yogurt

Directions:

Heat up a pan with some oil over medium heat, add garlic and onion, stir, cook for 10 minutes and transfer to a bowl. Add black pepper, garlic, parsley, mozzarella, parmesan and yogurt, stir well, stuff the mushroom caps with this mix, arrange them on a lined baking sheet, bake in the oven at 400 degrees F for 20 minutes and serve them as an appetizer.

Nutrition:

Calories 120, Fat 1 Fiber 3 Carbs 11

Protein 7

Mozzarella Cauliflower Bars

Jim Westphalen

Preparation Time: 10 minutes

Cooking time: 40 minutes

Servings: 12

Ingredients: ¼ cup egg whites

1 big cauliflower head, riced

½ cup low-fat mozzarella cheese, shredded

1 teaspoon Italian seasoning

Black pepper to the taste

Directions:

Spread the cauliflower rice on a lined baking sheet, cook in the oven at 375 degrees F for 20 minutes, transfer to a bowl, add black pepper, cheese, seasoning and egg whites, stir well, spread into a rectangle pan and press well on the bottom.

Introduce in the oven at 375 degrees F, bake for 20 minutes, cut into 12 bars and serve as a snack.

Nutrition:

Calories 140 - Fat 1 - Fiber 3 - Carbs 6 - Protein 6

Shrimp and Pineapple Salsa

Preparation Time: 10 minutes

Cooking time: 40 minutes

Servings: 4

Ingredients:

1-pound large shrimp, peeled and deveined

20 ounces canned pineapple chunks

1 tablespoon garlic powder

1 cup red bell peppers, chopped

Black pepper to the taste

Directions:

Place shrimp in a baking dish, add pineapple, garlic, bell peppers and black pepper, toss a

bit, introduce in the oven, bake at 375 degrees F for 40 minutes, divide into small bowls and serve cold.

Nutrition:

Calories 170

Fat 5

Fiber 4

Carbs 15

Protein 11

Strawberry Buckwheat Pancakes

Preparation Time: 20 minutes

Cooking time: 5 minutes

Servings: 4

Ingredients:

100g (3½oz) strawberries, chopped

100g (3½ oz.) buckwheat flour

1 egg

250mls (8fl oz.) milk

1 teaspoon olive oil

1 teaspoon olive oil for frying

Freshly squeezed juice of 1 orange

175 calories per serving

Directions:

Pour the milk into a bowl and mix in the egg and a teaspoon of olive oil. Sift in the flour to the liquid mixture until smooth and creamy. Allow it to rest for 15 minutes. Heat a little oil in a pan and pour in a quarter of the mixture (or to the size you prefer.)

Sprinkle in a quarter of the strawberries into the batter. Cook for around 2 minutes on each side. Serve hot with a drizzle of orange juice. You could try experimenting with other berries such as blueberries and blackberries

Nutrition:

Calories

Fat

Fiber

Carbs

Protein

Strawberry & Nut Granola

Preparation Time: 10 minutes

Cooking time: 50 minutes

Servings: 12

Ingredients:

200g (7oz) oats

250g (9oz) buckwheat flakes

100g (3½ oz.) walnuts, chopped

100g (3½ oz.) almonds, chopped

100g (3½ oz.) dried strawberries

1½ teaspoons ground ginger

1½ teaspoons ground cinnamon

120mls (4fl oz.) olive oil

2 tablespoon honey

Directions:

Combine the oats, buckwheat flakes, nuts, ginger and cinnamon. In a saucepan, warm the oil and honey. Stir until the honey has melted. Pour the warm oil into the dry ingredients and mix well. Spread the mixture out on a large baking tray (or two) and bake in the oven at 150C (300F) for around 50 minutes until the granola is golden. Allow it to cool. Add in the dried berries. Store in an airtight container until ready to use. Can be served with yogurt, milk or even dry as a handy snack.

Nutrition:

Calories 391

Fat 0

Fiber 6

Carbs 3

Protein 8

Chilled Strawberry & Walnut Porridge

Preparation Time: 10 minutes

Cooking time: 0 minutes

Servings: 1

Ingredients:

100g (3½ oz.) strawberries

50g (2oz) rolled oats

4 walnut halves, chopped

1 teaspoon chia seeds

200mls (7fl oz.) unsweetened soya milk

100ml (3½ FL oz.) water

Directions:

Place the strawberries, oats, soya milk and water into a blender and process until smooth. Stir in the chia seeds and mix well. Chill in the fridge overnight and serve in the morning with a sprinkling of chopped walnuts. It's simple and delicious.

Nutrition:

Calories 384 Fat 2

Fiber 5 Carbs 3 Protein7

Fruit & Nut Yogurt Crunch

Preparation Time: 5 minutes

Cooking time: 0 minutes

Servings: 1

Ingredients:

100g (3½ oz.) plain Greek yogurt

50g (2oz) strawberries, chopped

6 walnut halves, chopped

Sprinkling of cocoa powder

Directions:

Stir half of the chopped strawberries into the yogurt. Using a glass, place a layer of yogurt with a sprinkling of strawberries and walnuts, followed by another layer of the same until you reach the top of the glass. Garnish with walnuts pieces and a dusting of cocoa powder.

Nutrition:

Calories 296 Fat 4 Fiber 2 Carbs 5 Protein 9

Cheesy Baked Eggs

Preparation Time: 5 minutes

Cooking time: 15 minutes

Servings: 4

Ingredients:

4 large eggs

75g (3oz) cheese, grated

25g (1oz) fresh rocket (arugula) leaves, finely chopped

1 tablespoon parsley

½ teaspoon ground turmeric

1 tablespoon olive oil

Directions:

Grease each ramekin dish with a little olive oil.

Divide the rocket (arugula) between the ramekin dishes then break an egg into each one.

Sprinkle a little parsley and turmeric on top then sprinkle on the cheese.

Place the ramekins in a preheated oven at 220C/425F for 15 minutes, until the eggs are set and the cheese is bubbling.

Nutrition:

Calories 198

Fat 9

Fiber 3

Carbs 2

Protein 13

Green Egg Scramble

Preparation Time: 10 minutes

Cooking time: 5 minutes

Servings: 1

Ingredients:

2 eggs, whisked

25g (1oz) rocket (arugula) leaves

1 teaspoon chives, chopped

1 teaspoon fresh basil, chopped

1 teaspoon fresh parsley, chopped

1 tablespoon olive oil

Directions:

Mix the eggs together with the rocket (arugula) and herbs. Heat the oil in a frying pan and pour into the egg mixture. Gently stir until it's lightly scrambled. Season and serve.

Nutrition:

Calories 250 Fat 5 Fiber 7

Carbs 8 Protein 11

Spiced Scramble

Preparation Time: 10 minutes

Cooking time: 5 minutes

Servings: 1

Ingredients:

25g (1oz) kale, finely chopped

2 eggs

1 spring onion (scallion) finely chopped

1 teaspoon turmeric

1 tablespoon olive oil

Sea salt

Freshly ground black pepper

Directions:

Crack the eggs into a bowl. Add the turmeric and whisk them. Season with salt and pepper. Heat the oil in a frying pan, add the kale and spring onions (scallions) and cook until it has wilted. Pour in the beaten eggs and stir until eggs have scrambled together with the kale.

Nutrition:

Calories 259

Fat 3

Fiber 4

Carbs 3

Protein 9

Courgette Risotto

Preparation Time: 10 minutes

Cooking time: 5 minutes

Servings: 8

Ingredients:

2 tablespoons olive oil

4 cloves garlic, finely chopped

1.5 pounds Arborio rice

6 tomatoes, chopped

2 teaspoons chopped rosemary

6 courgettes, finely diced

1 ¼ cups peas, fresh or frozen

12 cups hot vegetable stock

1 cup chopped

Salt to taste - Freshly ground pepper

Directions:

Place a large heavy bottomed pan over medium heat. Add oil. When the oil is heated, add onion and sauté until translucent. Stir in the tomatoes and cook until soft. Stir in the rice and rosemary. Mix well. Add half the stock and cook until dry. Stir frequently. Add remaining stock and cook for 3-4 minutes. Add courgette and peas and cook until rice is tender. Add salt and pepper to taste. Stir in the basil. Let it sit for 5 minutes.

Nutrition:

Calories 406 - Fats 5 g - Carbohydrates 82 g - Proteins 14 g

Brown Basmati Rice Pilaf

Preparation Time: 10 minutes

Cooking time: 3 minutes

Servings: 2

Ingredients:

½ tablespoon vegan butter

½ cup mushrooms, chopped

½ cup brown basmati rice

2-3 tablespoons water

1/8 teaspoon dried thyme

Ground pepper to taste

½ tablespoon olive oil

¼ cup green onion, chopped

1 cup vegetable broth

¼ teaspoon salt

¼ cup chopped, toasted pecans

Directions:

Place a saucepan over medium-low heat. Add butter and oil. When it melts, add mushrooms and cook until slightly tender. Stir in the green onion and brown rice. Cook for 3 minutes. Stir constantly. Stir in the broth, water, salt and thyme. When it begins to boil, lower heat and cover with a lid. Simmer until rice is cooked. Add more water or broth if required. Stir in the pecans and pepper. Serve.

Nutrition:

Calories 189 - Fats 11 g - Carbohydrates 19 g - Proteins 4 g

Shakshuka

Preparation Time: 10 minutes

Cooking time:30 minutes

Servings: 1

Ingredients:

Chopped parsley - 1 tablespoon

Extra virgin olive oil - 1 teaspoon

Paprika - 1 teaspoon

Red onion – ½ cup (finely chopped)

Kale - 30g (stems removed and roughly chopped)

Garlic clove – 1 (finely chopped)

Celery - 30g (finely chopped)

Bird's eye chili – 1 (finely chopped)

Ground turmeric - 1 teaspoon

Ground cumin - 1 teaspoon

Tinned chopped tomatoes – 2 cups

Medium eggs – 2

Directions:

Place a small, deep-sided frypan over medium-low heat. Add the oil once hot, then add the chili, spices, celery, garlic, and onions. Fry for about 2 minutes. Add the tomatoes, then allow the sauce to simmer gently for approx. 20 min while stirring frequently. Add the kale to the pot and cook for another five minutes. Add a little water if the sauce gets too thick. Stir in the parsley once the sauce becomes nicely creamy. Create two little wells in the sauce, then break each egg into the wells. Reduce your heat to the lowest and cover the pan with a foil or with its lid. Allow the eggs to cook for about 10 minutes, or until the whites are firm and the yolks remain runny. Cook for another four minutes if you want the yolks to be firm. Serve immediately.

Nutrition:

calories 657 Protein 87

Fat 4 Sugar 6

Walnut and Date Porridge

Preparation Time: 10 minutes

Cooking time: 0 minutes

Servings: 1

Ingredients:

Strawberries – ½ cup (hulled)

Milk or dairy-free alternative - 200 ml

Buckwheat flakes – ½ cup

Medjool date – 1 (chopped)

Walnut butter - 1 teaspoon, or chopped walnut halves – 4

Directions:

Place the date and the milk in a pan, heat gently before adding the buckwheat flakes. Then cook until the porridge gets to your desired consistency. Add the walnuts, stir, then top with the strawberries. Serve.

Nutrition:

calories 254 Protein 65 Fat 4 Vitamin B

Vietnamese Turmeric Fish with Mango and Herbs Sauce

Preparation Time: 15 minutes

Cooking time: 30 minutes

Servings: 4

Ingredients:

For the Fish:

Coconut oil to fry the fish – 2 tablespoons

Fresh codfish, skinless and boneless – 1 ¼ lbs. (cut into 2-inch piece wide)

Pinch of sea salt, to taste

Fish Marinade:

Marinate the fish for a minimum of one hour or overnight

Chinese cooking wine - 1 tablespoon

Turmeric powder - 1 tablespoon

Sea salt - 1 teaspoon

Olive oil - 2 tablespoon

Minced ginger - 2 teaspoon

Mango Dipping Sauce

Juice of ½ lime

Medium-sized ripe mango – 1

Rice vinegar - 2 tablespoon

Dry red chili pepper - 1 teaspoon (stir in before serving)

Garlic clove – 1

Infused Scallion and Dill Oil

Fresh dill - 2 cups

Scallions - 2 cups (slice into long thin shape)

A pinch of sea salt, to taste.

Toppings

Nuts (pine or cashew nuts)

Lime juice (as much as you like)

Fresh cilantro (as much as you like)

Directions:

Add all the ingredients under "Mango Dipping Sauce" into your food processor. Blend until you get your preferred consistency.

Pan-Fry the Fish:

Add two tablespoons of coconut oil in a large non-stick frypan and heat over high heat. Once hot, add the pre-marinated fish. Add the slices of the fish into the pan individually - divide into batches for easy frying, if necessary.

Once you hear a loud sizzle, reduce the heat to medium-high.

Do not move or turn the fish until it turns golden brown on one side; then turn it to the other side to fry, about 5 minutes on each side. Add more coconut oil to the pan if needed — season with the sea salt.

Transfer the fish to a large plate. You will have some oil left in the frypan, which you will use to make your scallion and dill infused oil.

Make the Scallion and Dill Infused Oil:

Using the remaining oil in the frypan, set to medium-high heat, add 2 cups of dill, and 2 cups of scallions. Put off the heat after you have added the dill and scallions. Toss them gently for about 15 seconds, until the dill and scallions have wilted. Add a dash of sea salt to season.

Pour the dill, scallion, and infused oil over the fish. Serve with mango dipping sauce, nuts, lime, and fresh cilantro.

Nutrition:

Calories 234 Fat 23

Protein 76 Sugar 5

Chicken and Kale Curry

Preparation Time: 20 min

Cooking time: 1 hour

Servings: 3

Ingredients:

Boiling water – 250 ml

Skinless and boneless chicken thighs – 7 oz.

Ground turmeric – 2 tablespoons

Olive oil – 1 tablespoon

Red onions – 1 (diced)

Bird's eye chili – 1 (finely chopped)

Freshly chopped ginger – ½ tablespoon

Curry powder – ½ tablespoon

Garlic– 1 ½ cloves (crushed)

Cardamom pods – 1

Chopped tomatoes – ½ tin

Tinned coconut milk, light – 100 ml

Chicken stock – 2 cups

Tinned chopped tomatoes – 1 cup

Direction:

Place the chicken thighs in a non-metallic bowl, add one tablespoon of turmeric and one teaspoon of olive oil. Mix together and keep aside to marinate for approx. 30 minutes.

Fry the chicken thighs over medium heat for about 5 minutes until well cooked and brown on all sides. Remove from the pan and set aside.

Add the remaining oil into a frypan on medium heat.

Then add the onion, ginger, garlic, and chili. Fry for about 10 minutes until soft.

Add one tablespoon of the turmeric and half tablespoon of curry powder to the pan and cook for another 2 minutes. Then add the cardamom pods, coconut milk, tomatoes, and chicken stock. Allow simmering for thirty minutes. Add the chicken once the sauce has reduced a little into the pan, followed by the kale. Cook until the kale is tender and the chicken is warm enough. Serve with buckwheat. Garnish with the chopped coriander.

Nutrition:

Calories 313 Protein 13 Fat 6

Carbohydrate 23

Mediterranean Baked Penne

Preparation Time: 25 minutes

Cooking time: 1 hour 20 minutes

Servings: 8

Ingredients:

Extra-virgin olive oil – 1 tablespoon

Fine dry breadcrumbs – ½ cup

Small zucchini – 2 (chopped)

Medium eggplant – 1 (chopped)

Medium onion – 1 (chopped)

Red bell pepper – 1 (seeded and chopped)

Celery – 1 stalk (sliced

Garlic – 1 clove (minced)

Salt and freshly ground pepper to taste

Dry white wine – ¼ cup

Plum tomatoes – 1 X 28-ounce (drained and coarsely chopped, juice reserved)

Freshly grated Parmesan cheese – 2 tablespoons

Large eggs – 2 (lightly beaten)

Coarsely grated part-skim mozzarella cheese – 1 ½ cups

Dried penne rig ate or rigatoni – 1 pound

Directions:

Preheat your oven to 375 degrees F. apply nonstick spray on a 3-quart baking dish. Then coat the dish with ¼ cup of breadcrumbs, tapping out the excess.

Heat the oil in a large non-stick skillet over medium-high heat. Then add the onion, celery, bell pepper, eggplant, and zucchini. Cook for about 10 minutes, stirring occasionally, until smooth. Then add the garlic and cook for another minute. Add the wine, stir and cook for about 2 minutes, long enough for the wine to almost evaporate. Then add the juice and tomatoes. Bring to a simmer, then cook for about 10 to 15 minutes, until thickened, season with pepper and salt. Transfer to a large bowl and allow to cool. Pour water into a pot, add some salt, then allow to boil. Add the penne into the

boiling salted water to cook for about 10 minutes, until al dente. Drain and rinse the pasta under running water. Toss the pasta with the vegetable mixture, then stir in the mozzarella. Scoop the pasta mixture and place into the prepared baking dish. Drizzle the broken eggs evenly over the top. Mix the Parmesan and ¼ cups of breadcrumbs in a small bowl, then sprinkle evenly over the top of the dish.

Place the dish into the oven to bake for about 40 to 50 minutes, until bubbly and golden. Allow to stand for 10 min before you serve.

Nutrition:

Calories 372 Protein 45

Fat 8 Sugar 2

Prawn Arrabbiata

Preparation Time: 35 minutes

Cooking Time: 30 minutes

Servings: 1

Ingredients:

Raw or cooked prawns – 1 cup - Extra virgin olive oil - 1 tablespoon

Buckwheat pasta – ½ cup

For Arrabbiata Sauce

Chopped parsley - 1 tablespoon - Celery - ¼ cup (finely chopped)

Tinned chopped tomatoes – 2 cups

Red onion – 1/3 cup (finely chopped)

Garlic clove – 1 (finely chopped)

Extra virgin olive oil - 1 teaspoon

Dried mixed herbs - 1 teaspoon

Bird's eye chili – 1 (finely chopped)

White wine - 2 tablespoon (optional)

Directions:

Add the olive oil into your fry-pan and fry the dried herbs, celery, and onions over medium-low heat for about two minutes. Increase heat to medium, add the wine, and cook for another one min. Add the tomatoes to the pan and allow to simmer for about 30 minutes, over medium-low heat, until you get a nice creamy consistency. Add a little water if the sauce gets too thick. While the sauce is cooking, cook the pasta following the instruction on the packet. Drain the water once the pasta is done cooking, toss with the olive oil and set aside until needed. If using raw prawns, add them to your sauce and cook for another four minutes, until the prawns turn opaque and pink, then add the parsley. If using cooked prawns, add them at the same time with the parsley and allow the sauce to boil. Add the already cooked pasta to the sauce, mix them, and serve.

Nutrition:

Calories 321 -Protein 19 - Fat 2 - Carbohydrate

Potato Bites

Preparation Time: 10 minutes

Cooking time: 20 minutes

Servings: 3

Ingredients:

1 potato, sliced

2 bacon slices, already cooked and crumbled

1 small avocado, pitted and cubed

Cooking spray

Directions:

Spread potato slices on a lined baking sheet, spray with cooking oil, introduce in the oven at 350 degrees F, bake for 20 minutes, arrange on a platter, top each slice with avocado and crumbled bacon and serve as a snack.

Nutrition:

Calories 180

Fat 4

Fiber 1

Carbs 8

Protein 6

Eggplant Salsa

Preparation Time: 10 minutes

Cooking time: 10 minutes

Servings: 4

Ingredients:

1 and ½ cups tomatoes, chopped

3 cups eggplant, cubed

A drizzle of olive oil

2 teaspoons capers

6 ounces' green olives, pitted and sliced

4 garlic cloves, minced

2 teaspoons balsamic vinegar

1 tablespoon basil, chopped

Black pepper to the taste

Directions:

Heat a saucepan with the oil medium-high heat, add eggplant, stir and cook for 5 minutes.

Add tomatoes, capers, olives, garlic, vinegar, basil and black pepper, toss, cook for 5 minutes more, divide into small cups and serve cold.

Nutrition:

Calories 120 Fat 6Fiber 5

Carbs 9 Protein 7

Carrots and Cauliflower Spread

Preparation Time: 10 minutes

Cooking time: 40 minutes

Servings: 4

Ingredients:

1 cup carrots, sliced

2 cups cauliflower florets

½ cup cashews

2 and ½ cups water

1 cup almond milk

1 teaspoon garlic powder

¼ teaspoon smoked paprika

Directions:

In a small pot, mix the carrots with cauliflower, cashews and water, stir, cover, bring to a boil over medium heat, cook for 40 minutes, drain and transfer to a blender.

Add almond milk, garlic powder and paprika, pulse well, divide into small bowls and serve

Nutrition:

Calories 201 Fat 7 Fiber 4

Carbs 7 Protein 7

Black Bean Salsa

Preparation Time: 10 minutes

Cooking time: 0 minutes

Servings: 6

Ingredients:

1 tablespoon coconut aminos

½ teaspoon cumin, ground

1 cup canned black beans, no-salt-added, drained and rinsed

1 cup salsa

6 cups romaine lettuce leaves, torn

½ cup avocado, peeled, pitted and cubed

Directions:

In a bowl, combine the beans with the aminos, cumin, salsa, lettuce and avocado, toss, divide into small bowls and serve as a snack.

Nutrition:

Calories 181

Fat 4

Fiber 7

Carbs 14

Protein 7

Mung Sprouts Salsa

Preparation Time: 10 minutes

Cooking time: 0 minutes

Servings: 2

Ingredients: 1 red onion, chopped

2 cups Mung beans, sprouted

A pinch of red chili powder

1 green chili pepper, chopped

1 tomato, chopped

1 teaspoon chaat masala

1 teaspoon lemon juice

1 tablespoon coriander, chopped

Black pepper to the taste

Directions:

In a salad bowl, mix onion with Mung sprouts, chili pepper, tomato, chili powder, chaat masala, lemon juice, coriander and pepper, toss well, divide into small cups and serve.

Nutrition:

Calories 100 Fiber 1 Fat 3

Carbs 3 Protein 6

Sprouts and Apples Snack Salad

Preparation Time: 10 minutes

Cooking time: 0 minutes

Servings: 4

Ingredients:

1-pound Brussels sprouts, shredded

1 cup walnuts, chopped

1 apple, cored and cubed

1 red onion, chopped

For the salad dressing:

3 tablespoons red vinegar

1 tablespoon mustard

½ cup olive oil

1 garlic clove, minced

Black pepper to the taste

Directions:

In a salad bowl, mix sprouts with apple, onion and walnuts. In another bowl, mix vinegar with mustard, oil, garlic and pepper, whisk really well, add this to your salad, toss well and serve as a snack.

Nutrition:

Calories 120 Fat 2 Fiber 2

Carbs 8 Protein 6

Dijon Celery Salad

Preparation Time: 10 minutes

Cooking time: 0 minutes

Servings: 4

Ingredients:

5 teaspoons stevia

½ cup lemon juice

1/3 cup Dijon mustard

2/3 cup olive oil

Black pepper to the taste

2 apples, cored, peeled and cubed

1 bunch celery and leaves, roughly chopped

¾ cup walnuts, chopped

Directions:

In a salad bowl, mix celery and its leaves with apple pieces and walnuts.

Add black pepper, lemon juice, mustard, stevia and olive oil, whisk well, add to your salad, toss, divide into small cups and serve as a snack.

Nutrition:

Calories 125

Fat 2

Fiber 2

Carbs 7

Protein 7

Napa Cabbage Slaw

Preparation Time: 10 minutes

Cooking time: 0 minutes

Servings: 4

Ingredients:

½ cup of red bell pepper, cut into thin strips

1 carrot, grated

4 cups Napa cabbage, shredded

3 green onions, chopped

1 tablespoon olive oil

2 teaspoons ginger, grated

½ teaspoon red pepper flakes, crushed

3 tablespoons balsamic vinegar

1 tablespoon coconut aminos

3 tablespoons low-fat peanut butter

Directions:

In a salad bowl, mix bell pepper with carrot, cabbage and onions and toss.

Add oil, ginger, pepper flakes, vinegar, aminos and peanut butter, toss, divide into small cups and serve.

Nutrition:

Calories 160

Fat 10

Fiber 3

Carbs 10

Protein 5

Dill Bell Pepper Bowls

Preparation Time: 10 minutes

Cooking time: 0 minutes

Servings: 4

Ingredients:

2 tablespoons dill, chopped

1 yellow onion, chopped

1 pound multi colored bell peppers, cut into halves, seeded and cut into thin strips

3 tablespoons olive oil

2 and ½ tablespoons white vinegar

Black pepper to the taste

Directions:

In a salad bowl, mix bell peppers with onion, dill, pepper, oil and vinegar, toss to coat, divide into small bowls and serve as a snack.

Nutrition:

Calories 120

Fat 3

Fiber 4

Carbs 2

Protein 3

Baked Crispy Chicken

Preparation Time: 10 minutes

Cooking Time: 40 minutes

Servings: 12

Ingredients:

4 oz. pork rinds

Salt and pepper to taste

1 teaspoon oregano

1 ½ teaspoons thyme

1 teaspoon smoke paprika

½ teaspoon garlic powder

12 chicken legs - 2 oz. mayonnaise - 1 egg

3 tablespoons Dijon mustard

Directions:

Preheat your oven to 400 degrees F.

Grind pork rinds until they've turned into powdery texture.

Mix pork rinds with salt, pepper, oregano, thyme, paprika and garlic powder.

Spread mixture on a plate.

In a bowl, mix the mayo, egg and mustard.

Dip each chicken leg first into the egg mixture then coat with the pork rind mixture.

Bake in the oven for 40 minutes.

Nutrition:

Calories 359 - Total Fat 16.3g - Saturated Fat 4.7g

Cholesterol 158mg - Sodium 391mg - Total Carbohydrate 1.6g - Dietary Fiber 0.3g

Total Sugars 0.4g - Protein 49g -

Potassium 370mg

Italian Chicken

Preparation Time: 10 minutes

Cooking Time: 15 minutes

Servings: 4

Ingredients:

2 tablespoons olive oil - 1 ½ lb. chicken breast meat, sliced thinly

½ cup chicken broth - 1 cup heavy cream - 1 teaspoon Italian seasoning

½ cup Parmesan cheese - 1 teaspoon garlic powder - 1 cup spinach, chopped

½ cup sun dried tomatoes

Directions:

In a pan over medium heat, add olive oil.

Cook chicken for 4 to 5 minutes per side.

Transfer chicken on a plate.

Stir in the broth, cream, Italian seasoning, Parmesan cheese and garlic powder.

Simmer until the sauce has thickened.

Add the tomatoes and spinach.

Cook until the spinach has wilted.

Put the chicken back to the pan and serve.

Nutrition:

Calories 535 - Total Fat 29.4g

Saturated Fat 11g - cholesterol 199mg

Sodium 317mg

Total Carbohydrate 6.1g

Dietary Fiber 1g

Total Sugars 0.4g

Protein 60.3g

Potassium 783mg

Chicken & Carrots

Preparation Time: 15 minutes

Cooking Time: 20 minutes

Servings: 4

Ingredients:

1 ½ lb. carrots, peeled and sliced

1 onion, sliced into quarters

1 head garlic, top sliced off

4 tablespoons olive oil, divided

Salt and pepper to taste

1 tablespoon fresh rosemary, chopped

4 chicken thighs

Directions:

Preheat your oven to 425 degrees F. Arrange the onion and carrots on a single layer on a baking pan. Place the garlic in the middle of the tray. Drizzle half of the olive oil over the vegetables. Season with salt, pepper and rosemary. Coat the chicken with the remaining oil. Season with salt and pepper.

Bake in the oven for 20 minutes.

Nutrition:

Calories 532 - Total Fat 25.2g

Saturated Fat 5.1g - Cholesterol 130mg

Sodium 250mg - Total Carbohydrate 31.1g

Dietary Fiber 5.8g - Total Sugars 9.9g

Protein 46.1g - Potassium 1083mg

Lemon & Herb Chicken

Preparation Time: 20 minutes

Cooking Time: 60 minutes

Servings: 6

Ingredients:

1 whole chicken

4 tablespoons unsalted butter

3 lemons, sliced in half

½ bunch thyme

½ bunch rosemary

Salt and pepper to taste

Directions:

Preheat your oven to 425 degrees F. Cover the baking pan with foil. Put a roasting rack on top. Rub the chicken with butter.

Stuff the insides with lemon slices and herbs.

Season both inside and outside of chicken with salt and pepper.

Use twine to tie the chicken legs together.

Put the chicken on a roasting rack.

Roast for 40 minutes.

Reduce heat to 375 degrees F and roast until chicken is fully cooked.

Let chicken rest for 15 minutes before slicing and serving.

Nutrition:

Calories 504 -- Total Fat 36.1g - Saturated Fat 15g - Cholesterol 180mg

Sodium 216mg - Total Carbohydrate 4.3g - Dietary Fiber 1.8g

Total Sugars 0.8g - Protein 42.6g - Potassium 65mg

Chicken & Avocado Salad

Preparation Time: 5 minutes

Cooking Time: 15 minutes

Servings: 4

Ingredients:

Chicken

¼ cup water

2 boneless chicken thigh fillets

2 tablespoons olive oil

Salt and pepper to taste

1 teaspoon sweet chili powder

1 teaspoon dried thyme

4 cloves garlic

Salad

2 cups arugula

1 cup purslane leaves

1 cup basil leaves

½ cup fresh dill

½ cup cherry tomatoes, sliced in half

1 tablespoon olives

1 avocado, sliced

1 teaspoon sesame seeds

½ tablespoon olive oil

2 tablespoons avocado dressing

Directions:

Pour water into a skillet.

Cook chicken over medium low heat for 5 minutes.

Drizzle olive oil over the chicken

Season with the salt, pepper, thyme and chili powder.

Cook until golden, flipping several times to cook evenly.

Chop the chicken.

Arrange all the ingredients for the salad in a bowl.

Put the chicken on top of the salad.

Drizzle with the avocado dressing and olive oil.

Sprinkle sesame seeds on top.

Nutrition:

Calories 517

Total Fat 38.6g

Saturated Fat 6.4g Cholesterol 70mg

Sodium 368mg Total Carbohydrate 27.3g

Dietary Fiber 9.9g Total Sugars 7.2g

Protein 22g

Potassium 1102mg

Chicken Bowl

Preparation Time: 10 minutes

Cooking Time: 20 minutes

Servings: 4

Ingredients:

Salt and pepper to taste

2 teaspoons basil

2 teaspoon rosemary

2 teaspoons thyme

1 teaspoon paprika

2 lb. chicken breast meat, sliced into bite sized pieces

1 ½ cups broccoli florets

1 onion, chopped

1 cup tomatoes

1 zucchini, chopped

2 teaspoons garlic, minced

2 tablespoons olive oil

2 cups cauliflower rice

Directions:

Preheat your oven to 450 degrees F.

Cover your baking pan with foil. Set aside.

In a bowl, mix salt, pepper and spices.

Put the chicken and vegetables on a baking pan.

Sprinkle the spice mixture and garlic over the vegetables and chicken.

Drizzle olive oil on top.

Bake in the oven for 20 minutes.

Broil the chicken for 2 minutes.

Serve the chicken and vegetables in a bowl on top of cauliflower rice.

Nutrition:

Calories 558

Total Fat 19.1g Saturated Fat 4.4g

Cholesterol 206mg

Sodium 260mg

Total Carbohydrate 14.2g

Dietary Fiber 3.3g

Total Sugars 5.9g

Protein 80.3g

Potassium 1039mg

Chicken with Bacon & Ranch Sauce

Preparation Time: 10 minutes

Cooking Time: 20 minutes

Servings: 4

Ingredients:

4 chicken breasts - 1 teaspoon paprika

1 teaspoon garlic powder - 1 teaspoon onion powder

1 tablespoon avocado oil - 6 oz. cream cheese

1 tablespoon ranch seasoning powder

1 cup cheddar, grated

10 slices bacon, cooked and crumbled

2 tablespoons green onions, chopped

Directions:

Preheat your oven to 375 degrees F.

Season the chicken with the paprika, garlic powder and onion powder.

Pour the oil in a pan over medium heat.

Cook the chicken in a pan over medium heat.

Cook for 4 minutes per side.

In a bowl, mix the cream cheese and ranch seasoning.

Spread the cream cheese mixture on top of the chicken.

Top with the cheese.

Bake in the oven for 10 minutes.

Top with the bacon and green onion before serving.

Nutrition:

Calories 743 - Total Fat 48g – S

aturated Fat 20.2g - Cholesterol 235mg

Sodium 1523mg - Total Carbohydrate 4.1g - Dietary Fiber 0.5g

Total Sugars 0.8g -

Protein 70.3g - Potassium 738mg

Creamy Chicken & Mushroom

Preparation Time: 10 minutes

Cooking Time: 20 minutes

Servings: 4

Ingredients:

1 lb. chicken tenderloin

Salt and pepper to taste

2 tablespoons butter, divided

2 tablespoons olive oil, divided

½ lb. mushrooms, sliced

2 cloves garlic, crushed

¼ cup fresh parsley, chopped

2 tablespoons fresh thyme

1 cup chicken broth

½ cup heavy cream

¼ cup sour cream

Directions:

Season chicken with salt and pepper.

Add 1 tablespoon each of butter and olive oil in a pan. ear the chicken until brown on both sides. Set aside. Add the remaining oil and butter. Cook the mushrooms until crispy. Add the garlic, parsley and thyme. Pour in the broth. Stir in the cream and sour cream.

Simmer until the sauce has thickened.

Put the chicken back to the sauce.

Nutrition:

Calories 383 Total Fat 23g

Saturated Fat 10.1g

Cholesterol 122mg

Sodium 611mg

Total Carbohydrate 4.7g

Dietary Fiber 1.2g Total Sugars 1.3g

Protein 42.1g Potassium 304mg

Mozzarella Chicken

Preparation Time: 10 minutes

Cooking Time: 20 minutes

Servings: 4

Ingredients:

4 chicken breasts (boneless, skinless)

1 tablespoon Italian seasoning, divided

½ teaspoon onion powder

Salt and pepper to taste

1 teaspoon paprika

1 tablespoon olive oil

1 onion, chopped

4 cloves garlic, minced

1 fire roasted pepper, chopped

15 oz. tomato puree

2 tablespoons tomato paste

¾ cup mozzarella, shredded

1 tablespoons parsley, chopped

Directions:

Preheat your oven to 375 degrees F.

Season the chicken with 2 teaspoons Italian seasoning, onion powder, salt, pepper and paprika. Pour the oil in a pan over medium heat. Cook the chicken until brown on both sides. Set aside. Add the onion to the pan. Cook for 3 minutes. Add the garlic and pepper.

Cook for 1 minute. Add the tomato puree and tomato paste. Mix well. Stir in the remaining Italian sauce. Simmer for 4 minutes. Arrange the chicken on top of the sauce. Add mozzarella on top. Bake for 2 minutes.

Garnish with parsley before serving.

Nutrition:

Calories 387 Total Fat 16.2g

Saturated Fat 4.1g Cholesterol 130mg

Sodium 193mg Total Carbohydrate 15.8g

Dietary Fiber 3.3g Total Sugars 7.8g

Protein 44.7g Potassium 963mg

Chicken Parmesan

Preparation Time: 20 minutes

Cooking Time: 8 minutes

Servings: 2

Ingredients:

2 chicken breast fillets

1 tablespoon heavy whipping cream

1 egg

1 ½ oz. pork rinds, crushed

1 oz. Parmesan cheese, grated

Salt and pepper to taste

½ teaspoon garlic powder

½ teaspoon Italian seasoning

1 tablespoon ghee

½ cup tomato sauce

¼ cup mozzarella cheese, shredded

Directions:

Pound chicken fillet until flat.

In a bowl, mix the cream and egg.

Mix the pork rinds, Parmesan cheese, salt, pepper, garlic powder and Italian seasoning on another plate.

Dip the chicken fillet into the egg mixture.

Coat with the breading.

Add the ghee to a pan over medium heat.

Cook the chicken for 3 minutes per side.

Put the chicken to a baking pan.

Cover the top with tomato sauce and mozzarella cheese.

Broil for 2 minutes.

Nutrition:

Calories 589

Total Fat 33.9g

Saturated Fat 14.9g

Cholesterol 282mg

Sodium 1044mg

Total Carbohydrate 5g

Dietary Fiber 1g

Total Sugars 3.1g

Protein 65.3g

Potassium 602mg

Crab Melt

Preparation Time: 5 minutes

Cooking time: 20 minutes

Servings: 4

Ingredients:

2 zucchinis - A single tablespoon olive oil - 3 ounces of stalks from celery

3/4 cup of mayo

12 ounces of crab meat

A single red bell pepper

7 ounces of cheese (use shredded cheddar)

A single tablespoon of Dijon mustard

Direction:

Preheat your oven to 450.

Slice your zucchini lengthwise. Go for about a half-inch thick.

Add salt.

Let it sit for 15 minutes.

Pat it dries with a paper towel.

Place your slices on a baking sheet.

The baking sheet needs to be lined with parchment paper.

Brush olive oil on each side.

Finely chop the vegetables.

Mix with the other ingredients.

Apply mix to zucchini.

Bake for 20 minutes. Your top will be golden brown.

Nutrition:
Calories-742 - Fat-65 grams - Fiber-3 grams

Carbs-7 grams - Protein-30 grams

Spinach Frittata
Preparation Time: 10 minutes

Cooking time: 35 minutes,

Servings: 4

Ingredients:

5 ounces of diced bacon

2 tablespoons of butter

8 ounces of spinach that's fresh

8 eggs

A single cup of heavy whipping cream

5 ounces of shredded cheese

Directions:

Preheat your oven to 350 and grease a 9 by 9 baking dishes. Fry your bacon on a heat medium until it is crispy. Add your spinach and stir until it has wilted.

Remove pan from heat. Place it to the side. Whisk cream and eggs together and pour into the baking dish.

Add the spinach and bacon and pour the cheese on top.

Put in the middle of the oven.

Bake a half hour.

It should be set in the middle. The color on top should be golden brown.

Nutrition:

Calories: 661g - Fat: 59g - Fiber: 1g

Protein: 27 grams - Carbs: 4 grams

Halloumi Time
Preparation Time: 5 minutes

Cooking time: 15 minutes

Servings: 2

Ingredients

3 ounces of halloumi cheese that has been diced

2 chopped scallions

4 ounces of diced bacon

2 tablespoons of olive oil

4 tablespoons of chopped fresh parsley

4 eggs

Half a cup of pitted olives

Directions

In a frying pan on medium-high heat, heat the oil.

Fry the scallions, cheese, and bacon until they are nicely browned.

Get a bowl and whisk your eggs and parsley together.

Pour the egg mix into the pan over the bacon.

Lower heat. Add olives. Stir for 2 minutes.

Nutrition:

Calories: 663g Protein: 28g Carbs: 4g

Fat: 59g

Hash Browns
Preparation Time: 20 minutes

Cooking time: 10 minutes

Servings: 4

Ingredients:

3 eggs

A pound of cauliflower

Half a grated yellow onion

4 ounces of butter

Directions:

Rinse the cauliflower.

Trim it.

Grate it using a food processor.

Add it to a bowl.

Add everything and mix.

Set aside 10 minutes.

Melt a good amount of butter on medium heat.

You need a larger skillet.

Place the mix in the pan and flatten.

Fry for 5 minutes on each side. Don't burn it.

Nutrition:

Calories: 282 Carbs: 5g Protein: 7g

Fat: 26g

Poblano Peppers
Preparation Time: 5minutes

Cooking time: 15minutes

Servings: 2

Ingredients

A pound of grated cauliflower

3 ounces of butter

4 eggs

3 ounces of poblano peppers

A single tablespoon of olive oil

Half a cup of mayo

Directions:

Put your mayo in a bowl to the side.

Grate the cauliflower, including the stem.

Fry the cauliflower for 5 minutes in the butter.

Brush the oil on the peppers.

Fry them until you see the skin bubble a little.

Fry your eggs any way you like.

Servings with mayo.

Nutrition:

Calories: 898

Fat: 87g

Protein: 17g

Carbs: 9g

Salad with Butter

Preparation Time: 5minutes

Cooking time: 10minutes

Servings: 2

Ingredients:

10 ounces of goat cheese

A quarter cup of pumpkin seeds

2 ounces of butter

Tablespoons of balsamic vinegar

3 ounces of spinach (use baby spinach)

Directions:

Preheat oven to 400.

Put goat cheese in a baking dish that is greased.

Bake 10 minutes.

Toast pumpkin seeds in a frying pan that is dry. The temperature should be fairly high. They need some color, and they should start to pop.

Lower heat.

Add butter and simmer till it smells nutty and is golden brown.

Add vinegar and boil 3 minutes.

Turn off heat.

Spread the spinach on your plate and top with cheese and sauce.

Nutrition:

Calories: 824 Fat: 73g Protein: 37g Carbs: 3g

Mushroom Omelet

Preparation Time: 5minutes

Cooking time: 10minutes

Servings: 1

Ingredients:

4 sliced large mushrooms

A quarter chopped yellow onion

A single ounce of shredded cheese

An ounce of butter

3 eggs

Directions:

Crack the eggs and whisk them.

When smooth and frothy, they are good.

Melt butter over medium heat in a frying pan.

Add onions and mushrooms and stir until they become tender.

Pour the egg mix in. Surround the veggies.

When the omelet begins to get firm but is still a little raw on top, add cheese.

Carefully ease around the edges and fold in half. When it's golden brown underneath (turning this color), remove and plate it.

Nutrition:

Calories: 517g Protein: 26g Fat: 4g Carbs: 5g

Tuna Casserole

Preparation time 7minutes

Cooking time 20minutes

Serving: 4

Ingredients:

A single green bell pepper

5 ⅓ celery stalks

16 ounces of tuna in olive oil and drained

A single yellow onion

2 ounces of butter

A single cup of mayo

4 ounces of parmesan cheese freshly shredded

A single teaspoon of chili flakes

Directions:

Preheat your oven to 400.

Chop all of the bell peppers, onions, and celery finely before frying it in butter in a frying pan. They should be slightly soft.

Mix mayo and tuna with the flakes and cheese.

This should be done in a greased baking dish.

Add the veggies.

Stir.

Bake 20 minutes.

It should be golden brown.

Nutrition:

Calories: 953

Fat: 83g

Protein: 43g - Carbs: 5g

Goat Cheese Frittata

Preparation Time: 15minutes

Cooking time: 30minutes

Servings: 2

Ingredients:

4 ounces of goat cheese

5 ounces of mushrooms

3 ounces of fresh spinach

2 ounces of scallions

2 ounces of butter

Half a dozen eggs

Directions:

Preheat your oven to 350.

Crack the eggs and whisk before crumbling cheese in the mix.

Cut mushrooms into wedge shapes.

KETO COOKBOOK AFTER 50

Chop up the scallions. Melt the butter in a skillet that is oven proof and cook scallions and mushrooms over medium heat for 10 minutes. They will be golden brown (or should be). Add spinach and sauté two minutes. Pour egg mixture into the skillet. Place in the oven uncovered and bake 20 minutes. It should be golden brown in the center.

Nutrition:

Calories: 774 Fat: 67g Carbs: 6g
Protein: 35g

Pasta

Preparation Time: 5minutes

Cooking time: 1 minutes

Serving: 1

Ingredients:

A single large egg yolk

A single cup of mozzarella cheese that is part-skim low moisture and shredded

Directions:

In a bowl safe for the microwave, you will need to microwave the cheese for 60 seconds.

Stir until it's totally melted.

Allow to cool for 60 seconds.

Add in yolk and stir. It should make a yellow dough.

Place it on a flat surface that has been lined with parchment paper.

Place another paper over the dough.

Get a rolling pin and roll dough.

Remove the top piece when the dough is an eighth of an inch thick. Cut the dough into half-inch wide strips.

Put in the fridge for 6 hours. Put pasta in a pot of boiling water to cook and do not add salt. Cook for 60 seconds. Don't cook too long. Remove and run under cold water.

Separate the strands.

Nutrition:

Calories: 358

Fat: 22g

Protein: 33g- Carbs: 3g

Muffins

Preparation Time: 15 minutes

Cooking time: 10mins

Servings: 12

Ingredients:

5 whisked medium eggs

2 cups of whole nuts

Directions:

Preheat oven to 350.

Grease a muffin tray (12 cups)

Process the nuts in a food processor.

Whisk eggs and nut flour, you made in a bowl. Put in-tray. Bake 25 minutes. Stick should come out clean. Let cool.

Nutrition:

One muffin Calories: 117 Carbs: 4g

Protein: 6g Fat: 10g

Meaty Salad

Preparation Time: 5minutes

Cooking time: 10

Servings: 2

Ingredients:

3.5 ounces of salami slices

2 cups of spinach

A single avocado large and diced

2 tablespoons of olive oil

A single teaspoon of balsamic vinegar

Directions:

Toss it all together.

Nutrition:

Calories: 454

Carbs: 10g

Protein: 9g

Fat: 42g

Tomato Salad

Preparation Time: 10minutes

Cooking time: 5 minutes

Servings: 2

Ingredients:

A dozen small spear asparagus - 4 raw cherry tomatoes

A cup and a half of arugula

A single tablespoon of olive oil

A tablespoon of whole pieces pine nuts

A teaspoon of maple syrup

Tablespoon balsamic vinegar

2 tablespoon soft goat cheese

Directions:

Cut the tough ends off asparagus and throw away.

Place the asparagus in a pan of boiling water and cook 3 minutes.

Put in a bowl of ice-cold water right away.

Chill for 60 seconds.

Drain.

Put on a plate.

Slice your tomatoes in half, place on top of the greens. (arugula and asparagus)

Toss to combine.

Add the nuts to a pan that's dry and on a low heat toast for 2 minutes until it is lightly golden.

Add the syrup and vinegar along with the olive oil to a bowl and whisk, so they combine.

Drizzle the dressing on top and crumble your cheese.

Sprinkle the nuts over the top.

Nutrition:

Calories: 234 - Fat: 18g - Protein: 7g

Carbs: 7g

Shrimp with garlic

Preparation Time: 10 min

Cooking Time: 25 min

Servings: 2

Ingredients:

1 lb. shrimp

¼ teaspoon baking soda

2 tablespoons oil

2 teaspoon minced garlic

¼ cup vermouth

2 tablespoons unsalted butter

1 teaspoon parsley

Directions:

In a bowl toss shrimp with baking soda and salt, let it stand for a couple of minutes

In a skillet heat olive oil and add shrimp

Add garlic, red pepper flakes and cook for 1-2 minutes

Add vermouth and cook for another 4-5 minutes

When ready remove from heat and serve

Nutrition:

Calories: 289

Total Carbohydrate: 2 g

Cholesterol: 3 mg Total Fat: 17 g Fiber: 2 g

Protein: 7 g

Sodium: 163 mg

Sabich Sandwich

Preparation Time: 5 minutes

Cooking time: 15 minutes

Serving: 2

Ingredients:

2 tomatoes

Olive oil

½ lb. eggplant

¼ cucumber

1 tablespoon lemon

1 tablespoon parsley

¼ head cabbage

2 tablespoons wine vinegar

2 pita bread

½ cup hummus

¼ tahini sauce

2 hard-boiled eggs

Directions:

In a skillet fry eggplant slices until tender

In a bowl add tomatoes, cucumber, parsley, lemon juice and season salad

In another bowl toss cabbage with vinegar

In each pita pocket add hummus, eggplant and drizzle tahini sauce Top with eggs, tahini sauce

Nutrition:

Calories: 289 Total Carbohydrate: 2 g

Cholesterol: 3 mg Total Fat: 17 g

Fiber: 2 g Protein: 7 g

Sodium: 163 mg

Salmon with vegetables

Preparation Time: 10 minutes

Cooking time: 15 minutes

Serving: 4

Ingredients:

2 tablespoons olive oil - 2 carrots

1 head fennel - 2 squash

¼ onion - 1-inch ginger

1 cup white wine - 2 cups water

2 parsley sprigs - 2 tarragon sprigs

6 oz. salmon fillets - 1 cup cherry tomatoes

1 scallion

Directions:

In a skillet heat olive oil, add fennel, squash, onion, ginger, carrot and cook until vegetables are soft

Add wine, water, parsley and cook for another 4-5 minutes

Season salmon fillets and place in the pan

Cook for 4-5 minutes per side or until is ready Transfer salmon to a bowl, spoon tomatoes and scallion around salmon and serve

Nutrition:

Calories: 301 - Total Carbohydrate: 2 g - Cholesterol: 13 mg - Total Fat: 17 g

Fiber: 4 g

Protein: 8 g - Sodium: 201 mg

Crispy fish

Preparation Time: 5 minutes

Cooking time: 15 minutes

Serving: 4

Ingredients:

Thick fish fillets - ¼ cup all-purpose flour

1 egg - 1 cup bread crumbs

2 tablespoons vegetables - Lemon wedge

Directions:

In a dish add flour, egg, breadcrumbs in different dishes and set aside Dip each fish fillet into the flour, egg and then bread crumbs bowl Place each fish fillet in a heated skillet and cook for 4-5 minutes per side When ready remove from pan and serve with lemon wedges

Nutrition:

Calories: 189 Total Carbohydrate: 2 g

Cholesterol: 73 mg Total Fat: 17 g

Fiber: 0 g Protein: 7 g

Sodium: 163 mg

Moules marinieres

Preparation Time: 10 minutes

Cooking time: 30 minutes

Serving: 4

Ingredients:

2 tablespoons unsalted butter

1 leek - 1 shallot

2 cloves garlic

2 bay leaves

1 cup white win

2 lb. mussels

2 tablespoons mayonnaise

1 tablespoon lemon zest

2 tablespoons parsley

1 sourdough bread

Directions:

In a saucepan melt butter, add leeks, garlic, bay leaves, shallot and cook until vegetables are soft. Bring to a boil, add mussels, and cook for 1-2 minutes. Transfer mussels to a bowl and cover. Whisk in remaining butter with mayonnaise and return mussels to pot. Add lemon juice, parsley lemon zest and stir to combine

Nutrition:

Calories: 321

Total Carbohydrate: 2 g - Cholesterol: 13 mg

Total Fat: 17 g - Fiber: 2 g

Protein: 9 g - Sodium: 312 mg

Steamed mussels with coconut-curry

Preparation Time: 15 minutes

Cooking time: 20 minutes

Serving: 4

Ingredients:

6 sprigs cilantro - 2 cloves garlic

2 shallots - ¼ teaspoon coriander seeds

¼ teaspoon red chili flakes

1 teaspoon zest - 1 can coconut milk

1 tablespoon vegetable oil

1 tablespoon curry paste

1 tablespoon brown sugar

1 tablespoon fish sauce

2 lb. mussels

Directions:

In a bowl combine lime zest, cilantro stems, shallot, garlic, coriander seed, chili and salt

In a saucepan heat oil add, garlic, shallots, pounded paste and curry paste

Cook for 3-4 minutes, add coconut milk, sugar and fish sauce

Bring to a simmer and add mussels

Stir in lime juice, cilantro leaves and cook for a couple of more minutes. When ready remove from heat and serve

Nutrition:

Calories: 209 - Total Carbohydrate: 6 g Cholesterol: 13 mg - Total Fat: 7 g - Fiber: 2 g - Protein: 17 g - Sodium: 193 mg

Tuna noodle casserole

Preparation Time: 15 minutes

Cooking Time: 20 minutes

Serving: 4

Ingredient:

2 oz. egg noodles - 4 oz. fraiche

1 egg - 1 teaspoon cornstarch

1 tablespoon juice from 1 lemon

1 can tuna - 1 cup peas

¼ cup parsley

Directions:

Place noodles in a saucepan with water and bring to a boil. In a bowl combine egg, crème fraiche and lemon juice, whisk well. When noodles are cooked add crème fraiche mixture to skillet and mix well

Add tuna, peas, parsley lemon juice and mix well

When ready remove from heat and serve

Nutrition:

Calories: 214 Total Carbohydrate: 2 g

Cholesterol: 73 mg Total Fat: 7 g

Fiber: 2g Protein: 19 g Sodium: 308 g

Salmon burgers

Preparation Time: 10 minutes

Cooking Time: 15 minutes

Serving: 4

Ingredients:

1 lb. salmon fillets

1 onion

¼ dill fronds

1 tablespoon honey

1 tablespoon horseradish

1 tablespoon mustard

1 tablespoon olive oil

2 toasted split rolls

1 avocado

Directions:

Place salmon fillets in a blender and blend until smooth, transfer to a bowl, add onion, dill, honey, horseradish and mix well. Season with salt and pepper and form 4 patties. In a bowl combine mustard, honey, mayonnaise and dill. In a skillet heat oil add salmon patties and cook for 2-3 minutes per side. When ready remove from heat

Divided lettuce and onion between the buns

Place salmon patty on top and spoon mustard mixture and avocado slices

Serve when ready

Nutrition:

Calories: 189 - Total Carbohydrate: 6 g - Cholesterol: 3 mg Total Fat: 7 g - Fiber: 4 g - Protein: 12 g - Sodium: 293 mg

Seared scallops

Preparation Time: 15 minutes

Cooking time: 20 minutes

Serving: 4

Ingredients:

1 lb. sea scallops

1 tablespoon canola oil

Directions:

Season scallops and refrigerate for a couple of minutes

In a skillet heat oil, add scallops and cook for 1-2 minutes per side

When ready remove from heat and serve

Nutrition:

Calories: 283 Total Carbohydrate: 10 g

Cholesterol: 3 mg Total Fat: 8 g

Fiber: 2 g Protein: 9 g

Sodium: 271 mg

Black cod

Preparation Time: 15 minutes

Cooking time: 20 minutes

Serving: 4

Ingredients:

¼ cup miso paste

¼ cup sake

1 tablespoon mirin

1 teaspoon soy sauce

1 tablespoon olive oil

4 black cod filets

Directions:

In a bowl combine miso, soy sauce, oil and sake

Rub mixture over cod fillets and let it marinade for 20-30 minutes

Adjust broiler and broil cod filets for 10-12 minutes

When fish is cook remove and serve

Nutrition:

Calories: 231

Total Carbohydrate: 2 g

Cholesterol: 13 mg

Total Fat: 15 g

Fiber: 2 g

Protein: 8 g

Sodium: 298 mg

Miso-glazed salmon

Preparation Time: 10 minutes

Cooking time: 40 minutes

Serving: 4

Ingredients:

¼ cup red miso

¼ cup sake

1 tablespoon soy sauce

1 tablespoon vegetable oil

4 salmon fillets

Directions:

In a bowl combine sake, oil, soy sauce and miso

Rub mixture over salmon fillets and marinade for 20-30 minutes

Preheat a broiler

Broil salmon for 5-10 minutes

When ready remove and serve

Nutrition:

Calories: 198

Total Carbohydrate: 5 g

Cholesterol: 12 mg

Total Fat: 10 g

Fiber: 2 g

Protein: 6 g

Sodium: 257 mg

Arugula and sweet potato salad

Preparation Time: 10 minutes

Cooking time: 20 minutes

Serving: 4

Ingredients:

1 lb. sweet potatoes

1 cup walnuts

1 tablespoon olive oil

1 cup water

1 tablespoon soy sauce

3 cups arugula

Directions:

Bake potatoes at 400 F until tender, remove and set aside

In a bowl drizzle, walnuts with olive oil and microwave for 2-3 minutes or until toasted

In a bowl combine all salad ingredients and mix well

Pour over soy sauce and serve

Nutrition:

Calories: 189

Total Carbohydrate: 2 g

Cholesterol: 13 mg

Total Fat: 7 g

Fiber: 2 g

Protein: 10 g

Sodium: 301 mg

Nicoise salad

Preparation Time: 15 minutes

Cooking time: 10 minutes

Serving: 4

Ingredients:

1 oz. red potatoes

1 package green beans

2 eggs

½ cup tomatoes

2 tablespoons wine vinegar

¼ teaspoon salt

½ teaspoon pepper

½ teaspoon thyme

¼ cup olive oil

6 oz. tuna

¼ cup Kalamata olives

Directions:

In a bowl combine all ingredients together

Add salad dressing and serve

Nutrition:

Calories: 189

Total Carbohydrate: 2 g

Cholesterol: 13 mg

Total Fat: 7 g

Fiber: 2 g

Protein: 15 g

Sodium: 321 mg

Shrimp curry

Preparation Time: 15 minutes

Cooking time: 20 minutes

Serving: 4

Ingredients:

2 tablespoons peanut oil

¼ onion

2 cloves garlic

1 teaspoon ginger

1 teaspoon cumin

1 teaspoon turmeric

1 teaspoon paprika

¼ red chili powder

1 can tomatoes

1 can coconut milk

1 lb. peeled shrimp

1 tablespoon cilantro

Directions:

In a skillet add onion and cook for 4-5 minutes

Add ginger, cumin, garlic, chili, paprika and cook on low heat

Pour the tomatoes, coconut milk and simmer for 10-12 minutes

Stir in shrimp, cilantro, and cook for 2-3 minutes

When ready remove and serve

Nutrition:

Calories: 178

Total Carbohydrate: 3 g - Cholesterol: 3 mg

Total Fat: 17 g - Fiber: g - Protein: 9 g - Sodium: 297 mg

Salmon pasta

Preparation Time: 10 minutes

Cooking time: 25 minutes

Serving: 2

Ingredients:

5 tablespoons butter

¼ onion

1 tablespoon all-purpose flour

1 teaspoon garlic powder

2 cups skim milk - ¼ cup Romano cheese

1 cup green peas

¼ cup canned mushrooms

8 oz. salmon - 1 package penne pasta

Directions:

Bring a pot with water to a boil. Add pasta and cook for 10-12 minutes. In a skillet melt butter, add onion and sauté until tender. Stir in garlic powder, flour, milk and cheese. Add mushrooms, peas and cook on low heat for 4-5 minutes. Toss in salmon and cook for another 2-3 minutes. When ready serve with cooked pasta

Nutrition:

Calories: 211 - Total Carbohydrate: 7 g - Cholesterol: 13 mg

Total Fat: 18 g - Fiber: 3 g - Protein: 17 g - Sodium: 289 mg

Tilapia

Preparation Time: 10 minutes

Cooking time: 15 minutes

Serving: 2

Ingredients:

4 oz. fillets tilapia - ¼ cup all-purpose flour

1 tablespoon olive oil

2 tablespoons unsalted butter

Directions:

Season tilapia both sides with salt. Place each fillet into flour and coat

In a skillet heat olive oil and cook tilapia for 4-5 minutes per side. When ready remove from skillet and serve

Nutrition:

Calories: 201 - Total Carbohydrate: 2 g

Cholesterol: 6 mg - Total Fat: 17 g

Fiber: 2 g - Protein: 27 g

Sodium: 383 mg

Lime dressing

Preparation Time: 5 minutes

Cooking time: 5 minutes

Serving: 2

Ingredients:

8 oz. sour cream - ¼ adobo sauce

2 tablespoons lime juice

2 teaspoon lime zest - ¼ teaspoon cumin

¼ teaspoon chili powder

¼ teaspoon seasoning

Directions:

In a bowl add all ingredients and blend well. Pour dressing in a serving cup. Serve when ready

Nutrition:

Calories: 157 Total Carbohydrate: 2 g

Cholesterol: 29 mg Total Fat: 7 g

Fiber: 3 g Protein: 16 g Sodium: 393 mg

CHAPTER 12:

Soup Recipes

Teriyaki Sauce

Preparation Time: 10 minutes

Cooking time: 30 minutes

Servings: 1

Ingredients

7fl oz soy sauce - 7fl oz pineapple juice

1 teaspoon red wine vinegar

1-inch chunk of fresh ginger root, peeled and chopped

2 cloves of garlic

Directions

Place the ingredients into a saucepan, bring them to the boil, reduce the heat and simmer for 10 minutes. Let it cool then remove the garlic and ginger. Store it in a container in the fridge until ready to use. Use as a marinade for meat, fish and tofu dishes.

Nutrition:

Calories: 267,

Sodium: 33 mg, Dietary Fibre: 1.2 g,

Total Fat: 4.3 g, Total Carbs: 16.2 g,

Protein: 1.3 g.

Turmeric & Lemon Dressing

Preparation Time: 10 minutes

Cooking time: 30 minutes

Servings: 1

Ingredients

1 teaspoon turmeric

4 tablespoons olive oil

Juice of 1 lemon

Directions

Combine all the ingredients in bowl and serve with salads. Eat straight away.

Nutrition:

Calories: 125,

Sodium: 32 mg,

Dietary Fibre: 1.6 g,

Total Fat: 3.3 g,

Total Carbs: 16.3 g,

Protein: 1.5 g.

Garlic Vinaigrette

Preparation Time: 10 minutes

Cooking time: 30 minutes

Servings: 1

Ingredients

1 clove garlic, crushed

4 tablespoons olive oil

1 tablespoon lemon juice

Freshly ground black pepper

Directions

Simply mix all of the ingredients together. It can either be stored or used straight away.

Nutrition:

Calories: 104, Sodium: 35 mg,

Dietary Fibre: 1.3 g, Total Fat: 3.1 g,

Total Carbs: 16.2 g,Protein: 1.3 g.

The Salsa

Preparation Time: 20 minutes

Cooking time: 40 minutes

Servings: 1

Ingredients

One small tomato

One Thai chili, thinly sliced.

One teaspoon of caper, fine cut

Parsley - 2 teaspoons fine cut

1/4 of a lemon's juice

Directions

Remove the eye from the tomato to make the salsa and slice it finely, ensuring that the fluid remains in as much as possible. Combine chile, capers, lemon juice and parsley. You might mix it all in, but the end product is a little different.

Oven to 220 degrees Celsius (425 ° F), in one teaspoon, marinate the chicken breast with a little oil and lemon juice. Leave for five to ten minutes.

Then add the marinated chicken and cook on either side for about a minute, until pale golden, transfer to the oven (on a baking tray, if your pan is not ovenproof), 8 to 10 minutes or until cooked. Remove from the oven, cover with tape, and wait until eaten for five minutes.

Cook the kale for 5 minutes in a steamer in the meantime, add a little butter, fry the red onions and the ginger and then mix in the fluffy but not browned mix.

Cook the buckwheat with the remaining teaspoon of turmeric according to the package instructions. Eat rice, tomatoes and salsa. Eat together.

Nutrition:

Calories: 104,

Sodium: 33 mg,

Dietary Fibre: 1.6 g, - Total Fat: 4.3 g,

Total Carbs: 15.3 g,- Protein: 1.3 g.

Vinaigrette

Preparation Time: 10 minutes

Cooking time: 10 minutes

Servings: 2

Ingredients: A teaspoon of yellow mustard

A spoon of white wine vinegar

1 Teaspoon of honey

165 ml of prepared olive oil:

Directions

Mix mustard, vinegar and honey in a bowl. Add a small amount of olive oil and stir until the vinegar thickens. Season with salt and pepper.

Nutrition:

Calories: 1495, Sodium: 33 mg,

Dietary Fibre: 1.4 g, Total Fat: 4.3 g,

Total Carbs: 16.2 g, Protein: 1.5 g.

Walnut Vinaigrette

Preparation Time: 10 minutes

Cooking time: 10 minutes

Servings: 1

Ingredients

1 clove garlic, finely chopped

6 tablespoons olive oil

3 tablespoons red wine vinegar

1 tablespoon walnut oilSea salt - Freshly ground black pepper

Directions

Combine all of the ingredients in a bowl or container and season with salt and pepper. Use immediately or store in the fridge.

Nutrition:

Calories: 109,

Sodium: 33 mg, Dietary Fibre: 1.6 g,

Total Fat: 4.3 g, Total Carbs: 16.4 g,

Protein: 1.6 g.

Walnut & Mint Pesto

Preparation Time: 10 minutes

Cooking time: 10 minutes

Servings: 1

Ingredients

6 tablespoons fresh mint leaves

2oz walnuts - 2 cloves of garlic

3½oz Parmesan cheese

1 tablespoon lemon juice

Direction

Put all the ingredients into a food processor and blend until it becomes a smooth paste.

Nutrition:

Calories: 99, Sodium: 33 mg,

Dietary Fibre: 1.6 g, Total Fat: 4.4 g,

Total Carbs: 16.4 g, Protein: 1.6 g.

Parsley Pesto

Preparation Time: 10 minutes

Cooking time: 10 minutes

Servings: 1

Ingredients

3oz Parmesan cheese, finely grated

2oz pine nuts

6 tablespoons fresh parsley leaves, chopped

2 cloves of garlic - 2 tablespoons olive oil

Direction

Put all of the ingredients into a food processor or blend until you have a smooth paste.

Nutrition:

Calories: 104, Sodium: 32 mg,

Dietary Fibre: 1.6 g, Total Fat: 4.3 g,

Total Carbs: 16.2 g,Protein: 1.3 g.

Ras-el-Hanout hot sauce

Preparation Time: 10 minutes

Cooking time: 10 minutes

Servings: 2

Ingredients:

Olive oil

Lemon slices (juice)

Teaspoon honey

1½ teaspoons Ras el Hanout

1/ 2 red peppers, prepare:

Remove the seeds from the pepper.

Chopped peppers.

Directions

Put pepper in a bowl filled with lemon juice, honey and Ras-ElHanout and mix. Then add olive oil drop by drop while continuing to mix. Sweet and Sour Pot:

Nutrition:

Calories: 1495, Sodium: 33 mg,

Dietary Fibre: 1.6 g, Total Fat: 3.1 g,

Total Carbs: 16.5 g,Protein: 1.3 g.

Lemon Caper Pesto

Preparation Time: 10 minutes

Cooking time: 10 minutes

Servings: 1

Ingredients: 1 tablespoon lemon juice

6 tablespoons fresh parsley leaves

3 cloves of garlic - 2 tablespoons capers

2oz cashew nuts2 tablespoons olive oil

Serves 8: 95 calories per serving

Directions

Place all of the ingredients into a food processor and blitz until smooth. Add a little extra oil if necessary. Serve with pasta, vegetables or meat dishes.

Nutrition: Calories: 250, Sodium: 32 mg,

Dietary Fibre: 1.6 g, Total Fat: 4.1 g,

Total Carbs: 16.4 g,Protein: 1.5 g.

CHAPTER 13:

Desserts Recipes

Ice Cream with Avocado

Preparation Time: 10 minutes

Cooking time: 30 minutes

Servings: 6

Ingredients:

1 peeled and pitted the avocado

1½ teaspoon of vanilla paste

1 c.cm. Of coconut milk

2 tablespoons of almond butter

Drops of stevia

¼ teaspoon of Ceylon cinnamon

Directions:

Combine all ingredients in a food blender.

Blend until smooth.

Transfer the mixture into Popsicle molds and insert popsicle sticks.

Freeze for 4 hours or until firm.

Serve.

Nutrition:

Calories: 268 Total Carbohydrate: 9 g

Cholesterol: 42 mg Total Fat: 20 g

Fiber: 4 g Protein: 15 g

Delicious Brownies

Preparation Time: 10 minutes

Cooking time: 25 minutes

Servings: 4

Ingredients:

5 ounces of chocolate 86% (sugarless); melted

4 tablespoons of ghee, melted

3 eggs

½ cup of Swerve

¼ cup of mascarpone cheese

¼ cup of cocoa powder

Directions:

Take a big bowl; combine the melted chocolate with the ghee, eggs, swerve, cheese and cocoa. Whisk well, pour into a cake pan, introduce in the oven and cook at 375 degrees F for 25 minutes.

Cut into medium brownies and serve.

Nutrition:

Calories: 120

Total Carbohydrate: 9 g - Cholesterol: 43 mg

Total Fat: 27 g

Fiber: 6 g - Protein: 20 g

Chocolate Cake with Blueberry

Preparation Time: 10 minutes

Cooking time: 40 minutes

Servings: 8

Ingredients:

2 eggs, stripped into whites and yolks

25 g of cocoa powder

50 g of almond flour

20 g of flax flour

1 teaspoon. of sweetener (or to taste)

150 g of sour cream

50 g of vegetable oil

2 teaspoons. of baking powder

Vanilla or vanilla extract to taste

Directions:

Turn on the oven to 180 degrees.

Beat the squirrel to stable foam.

Beat yolks with sweetener.

Add sour cream and vegetable oil and mix.

Add all the dry ingredients and mix again, you can use a mixer.

Add proteins in two steps and mix them gently into the dough.

Use the form 16 cm in diameter.

Put in the oven for 25 minutes.

Cut the cake into two. You can soak them with a mixture of 1 tablespoon. of water and 1 teaspoon. of Liquor.

Nutrition:

Calories: 295

Total Carbohydrate: 9 g

Cholesterol: 52 mg

Total Fat: 27 g

Fiber: 2 g

Protein: 9 g

Chocolate Mousse

Preparation Time: 5 minutes

Cooking time: 5 minutes

Servings: 4

Ingredients:

1 tablespoon. of cocoa powder

2 oz. of cream cheese

2 oz. of butter

3 oz. of heavy whipping cream

Stevia to taste

Directions:

Melt the butter a bit and mix with the sweetener. Stir until blended. Add the cream cheese and cocoa powder and blend until smooth. Carefully whip heavy cream and gradually add to the mixture. Refrigerate it for 30 minutes.

Nutrition:

Calories: 227 Total Carbohydrate: 8 g

Cholesterol: 42 mg Total Fat: 36 g

Fiber: 2 g Protein: 4 g

Coconut Raspberry Cake

Preparation Time: 1 hour and 10 minutes

Cooking time: 10 Minutes.

Servings: 6

Ingredients:

For the biscuit:

2 cups almond flour - 1 egg

1 tablespoon of ghee, melted

½ teaspoon of baking soda

For the coconut layer:

1 cup of coconut milk

¼ cup of coconut oil, melted

3 cups coconut, shredded

1/3 cup of stevia

5 grams of food gelatin

For the raspberry layer:

1 cup of raspberries

1 teaspoon of stevia

3 tablespoons of chia seeds

5 grams of food gelatin

Directions:

In a bowl, combine the almond flour with the eggs, ghee and baking soda; stir well. Press on the bottom of the spring form pan, and introduce in the oven at 350 degrees F for 15 minutes. Leave aside to cool down.

Meanwhile, in a pan, combine the raspberries with 1-teaspoon stevia, chia seeds, and gelatin; stir, and cook for 5 minutes. Take off the heat, cool down and spread over the biscuit layer. In another small pan, combine the coconut milk with the coconut, oil, gelatin, 1/3 cup stevia; stir for 1-2 minutes. Take off the heat, cool down and spread over the coconut milk. Cool the cake in the fridge for 1 hour, slice and serve.

Nutrition:

Calories: 221 Total Carbohydrate: 9 g

Cholesterol: 32 mg Total Fat: 12 g

Fiber: 2 g Protein: 7 g

Chickpea Choco Slices

Preparation Time: 10 minutes

Cooking time: 50 minutes

Servings: 12 slices, 2 per serving

Ingredients:

400g can chickpeas,

Rinsed, drained 250g almond butter

70ml maple syrup

15ml vanilla paste

1 pinch salt

2g baking powder

2g baking soda

40g vegan chocolate chips

Directions:

Preheat oven to 180C/350F. Grease large baking pan with coconut oil.

Combine chickpeas, almond butter, maple syrup, vanilla, salt, baking powder, and baking soda in a food blender. Blend until smooth. Stir in half the chocolate chips- Spread the batter into the prepared baking pan. Sprinkle with reserved chocolate chips. Bake for 45-50 minutes or until an inserted toothpick comes out neat. Appease on a wire rack for twenty minutes. slice and serve.

Nutrition:

Calories: 426

Total Fat: 27.2g - Total Carbohydrate: 39.2g

Dietary Fiber: 4.9g - Total Sugars: 15.7g

Protein: 10g

Sweet Green Cookies

Preparation Time: 10 minutes

Cooking time: 30 minutes

Servings: 12 cookies, 3 per serving

Ingredients:

165g green peas

80g chopped Medjool dates

60g silken tofu, mashed

100g almond flour

1 teaspoon baking powder

12 almonds

Directions:

Preheat oven to 180C/350F.

Combine peas and dates in a food processor.

Process until the thick paste is formed.

Transfer the pea mixture into a bowl. Stir in tofu, almond flour, and baking powder.

Shape the mixture into 12 balls. Arrange balls onto baking sheet, lined with parchment paper. Flatten each ball with oiled palm. Insert an almond into each cookie. Bake the cookies for twenty-five to thirty minutes or until gently golden. Cool on a wire rack before serving.

Nutrition:

Calories: 221 Total Fat: 10.3g

Total Carbohydrate: 26.2g

Dietary Fiber: 6g - Total Sugars: 15.1g

Protein: 8.2g

Chickpea Cookie Dough

Preparation Time: 10 minutes

Cooking time: 0 minutes

Servings: 4

Ingredients:

400g can chickpeas, rinsed, drained

130g smooth peanut butter

10ml vanilla extract

½ teaspoon cinnamon

10g chia seeds

40g quality dark Vegan chocolate chips

Direction:

Drain chickpeas in a colander.

Remove the skin from the chickpeas.

Place chickpeas, peanut butter, vanilla, cinnamon, and chia in a food blender.

Blend until smooth.

Stir in chocolate chips and divide among four serving bowls.

Serve.

Nutrition:

Calories: 376

Total Fat: 20.9g

Total Carbohydrate: 37.2g

Dietary Fiber: 7.3g

Total Sugars: 3.3g

Protein: 14.2g

Banana Bars

Preparation Time: 10 minutes

Cooking time: 30 minutes

Servings: 8

Ingredients:

130g smooth peanut butter

60ml maple syrup

1 banana, mashed

45ml water

15g ground flax seeds

95g cooked quinoa

25g chia seeds

5ml vanilla

90g quick cooking oats

55g whole-wheat flour

5g baking powder

5g cinnamon

1 pinch salt

Topping:

5ml melted coconut oil

30g vegan chocolate, chopped

Directions:

Preheat oven to 180C/350F.

Line 16cm baking dish with parchment paper.

Put together water and flax seeds in a small bowl. Place aside 10 minutes.

In a separate bowl, combine peanut butter, maple syrup, and banana. Fold in the flax seed's mixture.

Once you have a smooth mixture, stir in quinoa, chia seeds, vanilla extract, oat, whole-wheat flour, baking powder, cinnamon, and salt.

Pour the batter into prepared baking dish. Cut into 8 bars.

Bake the bars for 30 minutes. In the meantime, make the topping; combine chocolate and coconut oil in a heatproof bowl. Set over simmering water, until melted. Remove the bars from the oven. Place on a wire rack for 15 minutes to cool.

Remove the bars from the baking dish, and drizzle with chocolate topping. Serve.

Nutrition:

Calories: 278 Total Fat: 11.9g

Total Carbohydrate: 35.5g

Dietary Fiber: 5.8g Total Sugars: 10.8g

Protein: 9.4g

Protein Donuts

Preparation Time: 5 minutes

Cooking Time: 20 minutes

Servings: 10 donuts, 2 per serving

Ingredients:

85g coconut flour

110g vanilla flavored germinated brown rice protein powder

25g almond flour

50g maple sugar

30ml melted coconut oil

8g baking powder

115ml soy milk

½ teaspoon apple cider vinegar

½ teaspoon vanilla paste

½ teaspoon cinnamon

30ml organic applesauce

Additional:

30g powdered coconut sugar

10g cinnamon

Directions:

Add all the dried ingredients in a large cup.

In a separate bowl, whisk the milk with applesauce, coconut oil, and cider vinegar.

Fold the wet ingredients into dry and stir until blended thoroughly.

Heat oven to 180C/350F and grease 10-hole donut pan. Spoon the prepared batter into greased donut pan. Bake the donuts for 15-20 minutes.

Sprinkle with coconut sugar and cinnamon while the donuts are still warm, Serve warm.

Nutrition:

Calories: 270 Total Fat: 9.3g

Total Carbohydrate: 28.4g

Dietary Fiber: 10.2g Total Sugars: 10.1g

Protein: 20.5g

Lentil Balls

Preparation Time: 10 minutes

Cooking time: 0 minutes

Servings: 16 balls, 2 per serving

Ingredients:

150g cooked green lentils

10ml coconut oil

5g coconut sugar

180g quick cooking oats

40g unsweetened coconut, shredded

40g raw pumpkin seeds

110g peanut butter

40ml maple syrup

Directions:

Add all ingredients in a large bowl, as listed.

Shape the mixture into 16 balls.

Arrange the balls onto a plate, lined with parchment paper.

Refrigerate 30 minutes.

Serve.

Nutrition:

Calories: 305

Total Fat: 13.7g

Total Carbohydrate: 35.4g

Dietary Fiber: 9.5g

Total Sugars: 6.3g

Protein: 12.6g

Homemade granola

Preparation Time: 10 minutes

Cooking time: 24 minutes

Servings: 8

Ingredients:

270g rolled oats

100g coconut flakes

40g pumpkin seeds

80g hemp seeds

30ml coconut oil

70ml maple syrup

50g Goji berries

Direction:

Add all ingredients on a large baking sheet.

Preheat oven to 180C°/350F.

Bake the granola for 12 minutes. Remove from the oven and stir.

Bake an additional 12 minutes.

Serve at room temperature.

Nutrition:

Calories: 344

Total Fat: 17.4g

Total Carbohydrate: 39.7g

Dietary Fiber: 5.8g

Total Sugars: 12.9g

Protein: 9.9g

Cookie Almond Balls

Preparation Time: 15 minutes

Cooking time: 0 minutes

Servings: 16 balls, 2 per serving

Ingredients:

100g almond meal

60g vanilla flavored rice protein powder

80g almond butter or any nut butter

10 drops Stevia

15ml coconut oil

15g coconut cream

40g vegan chocolate chips

Directions:

Combine almond meal and protein powder in a large bowl.

Fold in almond butter, Stevia, coconut oil, and coconut cream.

If the mixture is too crumbly, add some water. Fold in chopped chocolate and stir until combined.

Shape the mixture into 16 balls.

You can additionally roll the balls into almond flour.

Serve.

Nutrition:

Calories: 132 Total Fat: 8.4g

Total Carbohydrate: 6.7g

Dietary Fiber: 2.2g Total Sugars: 3.1g

Protein: 8.1g

Spiced Dutch Cookies

Preparation Time: 20 minutes

Cooking time: 8 minutes

Servings: 6

Ingredients: 180g almond flour

55ml coconut oil, melted

60g rice protein powder, vanilla flavor

1 banana, mashed 40g Chia seeds

Spice mix: 15g allspice

1 pinch white pepper

1 pinch ground coriander seeds

1 pinch ground mace

Directions:

Preheat oven to 190C/375F.

Soak chia seeds in ½ cup water. Place aside 10 minutes. Mash banana in a large bowl.

Fold in almond flour, coconut oil, protein powder, and spice mix. Add soaked chia seeds and stir to combine. Stir until the dough is combined and soft. If needed add 1-2 tablespoons water.

Roll the dough to 1cm thick. Cut out cookies. Arrange the cookies onto baking sheet, lined with parchment paper. Bake 7-8 minutes. Serve at room temperature.

Nutrition:

Calories: 278 - Total Fat: 20g –

Total Carbohydrate: 13.1g

Dietary Fiber: 5.9g - Total Sugars: 2.4g

Protein: 13.1g

Smoked salmon with cheese sauce

Preparation Time: 10 minutes

Cooking time: 20 minutes

Serving: 4

Ingredients:

8 leeks

1 lb. salmon slices

200g cheddar

2 oz. butter

2 oz. plain flour

400 ml milk

2 egg yolks

1 teaspoon mustard

1 teaspoon dill

Salt

Directions:

In a pan bring water to a boil, add leeks and cook for 5-6 minutes. When the leeks are cooked remove from the pan and place them in a baking dish. Add salmon over the leeks. In a pan melt butter, add flour and mix well. Whisk in milk and simmer for 2-3 minutes. Cook salmon fillets in mixture and set aside. In a bowl beat egg yolk, mustard, salt and pour over salmon

Nutrition:

Calories: 278

Total Fat: 20g - Total Carbohydrate: 13.1g

- Dietary Fiber: 5.9g

Total Sugars: 2.4g - Protein: 13.1g

Keto Frosty

Preparation Time: 45 minutes

Cooking Time: 0 minute

Servings: 4

Ingredients:

1 ½ cups heavy whipping cream

2 tablespoons cocoa powder (unsweetened)

3 tablespoons Swerve

1 teaspoon pure vanilla extract

Salt to taste

Directions:

In a bowl, combine all the ingredients.

Use a hand mixer and beat until you see stiff peaks forming.

Place the mixture in a Ziploc bag.

Freeze for 35 minutes.

Serve in bowls or dishes.

Nutrition:

Calories 164 Total Fat 17g

Saturated Fat 10.6g

Cholesterol 62mg

Sodium 56mg

Total Carbohydrate 2.9g

Dietary Fiber 0.8g

Total Sugars 0.2g

Protein 1.4g

Potassium 103mg

Keto Shake

Preparation Time: 15 minutes

Cooking Time: 0 minute

Serving: 1

Ingredients:

¾ cup almond milk

½ cup ice

2 tablespoons almond butter

2 tablespoons cocoa powder (unsweetened)

2 tablespoons Swerve

1 tablespoon chia seeds

2 tablespoons hemp seeds

½ tablespoon vanilla extract

Salt to taste

Directions:

Blend all the ingredients in a food processor.

Chill in the refrigerator before serving.

Nutrition:

Calories 104

Total Fat 9.5g

Saturated Fat 5.1g

Cholesterol 0mg

Sodium 24mg

Total Carbohydrate 3.6g

Dietary Fiber 1.4g - Total Sugars 1.1g

Protein 2.9g

Potassium 159mg

Keto Fat Bombs

Preparation Time: 30 minutes

Cooking Time: 0 minute

Servings: 10

Ingredients:

8 tablespoons butter

¼ cup Swerve

½ teaspoon vanilla extract

Salt to taste

2 cups almond flour

2/3 cup chocolate chips

Directions:

In a bowl, beat the butter until fluffy.

Stir in the sugar, salt and vanilla.

Mix well.

Add the almond flour.

Fold in the chocolate chips.

Cover the bowl with cling wrap and refrigerate for 20 minutes.

Create balls from the dough.

Nutrition:

Calories 176

Total Fat 15.2g

Saturated Fat 8.4g - Cholesterol 27mg

Sodium 92mg

Total Carbohydrate 12.9g - Dietary Fiber 1g - Total Sugars 10.8g

Protein 2.2g - Potassium 45mg

Avocado Ice Pops

Preparation Time: 20 minutes

Cooking Time: 0 minute

Servings: 10

Ingredients:

3 avocados

¼ cup lime juice

3 tablespoons Swerve

¾ cup coconut milk

1 tablespoon coconut oil

1 cup keto friendly chocolate

Directions:

Add all the ingredients except the oil and chocolate in a blender. Blend until smooth. Pour the mixture into the popsicle mold.

Freeze overnight. In a bowl, mix oil and chocolate chips.

Melt in the microwave. And then let cool.

Dunk the avocado popsicles into the chocolate before serving.

Nutrition:

Calories 176 Total Fat 17.4g

Saturated Fat 7.5g

Cholesterol 0mg - Sodium 6mg

Total Carbohydrate 10.8g –

 Dietary Fiber 4.5g

Total Sugars 5.4g - Protein 1.6g

Potassium 341mg

Carrot Balls

Preparation Time: 1 hour and 10 minutes

Cooking Time: 0 minute

Servings: 8

Ingredients:

8 oz. block cream cheese

¾ cup coconut flour

½ teaspoon pure vanilla extract

1 teaspoon stevia

¼ teaspoon ground nutmeg

1 teaspoon cinnamon

1 cup carrots, grated

1/2 cup pecans, chopped

1 cup coconut, shredded

Directions:

Use a hand mixer to beat the cream cheese, coconut flour, vanilla, stevia, nutmeg and cinnamon. Fold in the carrots and pecans.

Form into balls. Refrigerate for 1 hour.

Roll into shredded coconut before serving.

Nutrition:

Calories 390

Total Fat 35g - Saturated Fat 17g

Cholesterol 60mg - Sodium 202mg

Total Carbohydrate 17.2g - Dietary Fiber 7.8g

Total Sugars 6g - Protein 7.8g

Potassium 154mg -

Coconut Crack Bars

Preparation Time: 2 minutes

Cooking Time: 3 minutes

Servings: 20

Ingredients:

3 cups coconut flakes (unsweetened)

1 cup coconut oil

¼ cup maple syrup

Directions:

Line a baking sheet with parchment paper.

Put coconut in a bowl.

Add the oil and syrup.

Mix well.

Pour the mixture into the pan.

Refrigerate until firm.

Slice into bars before serving.

Nutrition:

Calories 147

Total Fat 14.9g

Saturated Fat 13g

Cholesterol 0mg

Sodium 3mg

Total Carbohydrate 4.5g

Dietary Fiber 1.1g

Total Sugars 3.1g

Protein 0.4g

Potassium 51mg

Strawberry Ice Cream

Preparation Time: 1 hour and 20 minutes

Cooking Time: 0 minute

Servings: 4

Ingredients:

17 oz. coconut milk

16 oz. frozen strawberries

¾ cup Swerve

½ cup fresh strawberries

Directions:

Put all the ingredients except fresh strawberries in a blender.

Pulse until smooth.

Put the mixture in an ice cream maker.

Use ice cream maker according to directions.

Add the fresh strawberries a few minutes before the ice cream is done.

Freeze for 1 hour before serving.

Nutrition:

Calories 320 Total Fat 28.8g

Saturated Fat 25.5g

Cholesterol 0mg

Sodium 18mg

Total Carbohydrate 25.3g

Dietary Fiber 5.3g

Total Sugars 19.1g

Protein 2.9g

Potassium 344mg

Key Lime Pudding

Preparation Time: 20 minutes

Cooking Time: 1 hour and 15 minutes

Servings: 2

Ingredients:

1 cup hot water

2/4 cup erythrytol syrup

6 drops stevia

1 teaspoon almond extract

1 teaspoon vanilla extract

¼ teaspoon Xanthan gum powder

2 ripe avocados, sliced

1 ½ oz. lime juice

3 tablespoons coconut oil

Salt to taste

Directions:

Add water, erythritol, stevia, almond extract and vanilla extract to a pot.

Bring to a boil.

Simmer until the syrup has been reduced and has thickened.

Turn the heat off.

Add the gum powder.

Mix until thickened.

Add the avocado into a food processor.

Add the rest of the ingredients.

Pulse until smooth.

Place the mixture in ramekins.

Refrigerate for 1 hour.

Pour the syrup over the pudding before serving.

Nutrition:

Calories 299 Total Fat 29.8g

Saturated Fat 12.9g

Cholesterol 0mg

Sodium 47mg Total Carbohydrate 9.7g

Dietary Fiber 6.8g

Total Sugars 0.8g Protein 2g

Potassium 502mg

Chicken rolls with pesto

Preparation Time: 20 minutes

Cooking time: 30 minutes

Servings: 1

Ingredients:

Tablespoon pine nuts

Yeast tablets

Garlic cloves (chopped)

Fresh basil

Olive oil

Chicken breast ready to slice:

Preheat the oven to 175 ° C.

Place the pine nuts in a dry pan and heat to a golden brown over medium heat for 3 minutes. Place on a plate and set aside.

Place pine nuts, yeast flakes and garlic in a food processor and grind finely.

Add basil and oil and mix briefly until you get pesto.

Directions

Season with salt and pepper.

Place each piece of the chicken breast between 2 pieces of plastic wrap. 7 Roll in a frying pan or pasta until the chicken breasts grow out.

0.6 cm thick.

Remove the plastic wrap, then apply pesto to the chicken.

Roll up the chicken breast and tie it with the cocktail skewers.

Season with salt and pepper.

Dissolve the coconut oil in the pan and use a high temperature to brown all sides of the chicken skin.

Place the chicken rolls on a baking sheet, place in the oven, and bake for 15 to 20 minutes, until cooked.

Slice it diagonally and serve it with other pesto sauce. It was served with tomato salad.

Nutrition:

Calories: 150,

Sodium: 33 mg,

Dietary Fibre: 1.6 g,

Total Fat: 4.3 g,

Total Carbs: 15.4 g,

Protein: 1.6 g.

Sweet and sour sauce:

Preparation Time: 10 minutes

Cooking time: 10 minutes

Servings: 1

Ingredients

Apple cider vinegar

1/2 tablespoon tomato paste

A teaspoon of coconut amino acid

Bamboo spoon

Water treatment

Chopped vegetables.

Directions

Mix kudzu powder with five tablespoons of cold water to make a paste.

Then put all the other spices in the pot, then add the kudzu paste.

Melt coconut oil in a pan and fry onions.

Add green pepper, cabbage, cabbage and bean sprouts, then cook until the vegetables are tender.

Add pineapple and cashew nuts and mix a few times.

Just pour a little spice into the pot.

Nutrition:

Calories: 3495, Sodium: 33 mg,

Dietary Fibre: 1.4 g, Total Fat: 4.5 g,

Total Carbs: 16.5 g,Protein: 1.7 g.

Coconut Curry Cauliflower Soup

Preparation Time: 10 minutes

Cooking Time: 25 minutes

Servings: 10

Ingredients:

2 tablespoons olive oil

1 onion, chopped

3 tablespoons yellow curry paste

2 heads cauliflower, sliced into florets

32 oz. vegetable broth

1 cup coconut milk

Minced fresh cilantro

Directions:

In a pan over medium heat, add the oil.

Cook onion for 3 minutes. Stir in the curry paste and cook for 2 minutes. Add the cauliflower florets. Pour in the broth. Increase the heat to high and bring to a boil.

Lower the heat to medium. Cook while covered for 20 minutes. Add the coconut milk and cook for an additional minute.

Puree in a blender.

Garnish with fresh cilantro.

Nutrition:

Calories 138 Total Fat 11.8g Saturated Fat 5.6g Cholesterol 0mg Sodium 430mg

Total Carbohydrate 6.4g Dietary Fiber 3g Total Sugars 2.8g Protein 3.6g

Potassium 318mg

Mexican Soup

Preparation Time: 5 minutes

Cooking Time: 15 minutes

Servings: 4

Ingredients:

2 teaspoons olive oil

1 lb. chicken thighs (skinless and boneless), sliced into smaller pieces

1 tablespoon taco seasoning

1 cup frozen corn

1 cup salsa

32 oz. chicken broth

Directions:

In a pan over medium heat, add oil. Cook chicken for 7 minutes, stirring frequently. Add the taco seasoning and mix well. Add the rest of the ingredients. Bring to a boil. Reduce heat to low and simmer for 5 minutes. Remove fat before serving.

Nutrition:

Calories 322

Total Fat 12.6g

Saturated Fat 3.1g

Cholesterol 101mg

Sodium 1214mg

Total Carbohydrate 12.2g -

Dietary Fiber 2.1g

Total Sugars 3.9g -

Protein 39.6g - Potassium 768mg

Roasted Tomato Soup

Preparation Time: 20 minutes

Cooking Time: 25 minutes

Servings: 6

Ingredients:

Cooking spray

3 ½ lb. tomatoes, sliced into half

1 onion, sliced into wedges

2 cloves garlic, sliced in half

2 tablespoons olive oil

Salt and pepper to taste

2 tablespoons fresh thyme leaves

12 fresh basil leaves

Directions:

Preheat your oven to 400 degrees F. Put the onion, garlic and tomatoes on a baking pan coated with cooking spray. Drizzle vegetables with olive oil and toss. Season with salt, pepper and thyme. Roast for 30 minutes. Place the tomato mixture and basil leaves in a blender. Pulse until smooth.

Nutrition:

Calories 99

Total Fat 5.3g Saturated Fat 0.8g

 Cholesterol 0mg

Sodium 14mg

Total Carbohydrate 13g Dietary Fiber 4g

Total Sugars 7.8g Protein 2.7g

Potassium 668mg

Squash Soup

Preparation Time: 15 minutes

Cooking Time: 20 minutes

Servings: 6

Ingredients:

5 leeks, sliced

2 tablespoons butter

4 cups chicken broth

¼ teaspoon dried thyme

4 cups butternut squash, peeled and cubed

¼ teaspoon pepper

2 cups cheddar cheese, shredded

1 green onion, thinly sliced

¼ cup sour cream

Directions:

In a pan over medium heat, sauté the leeks in butter. Add the broth, thyme, squash and pepper. Bring to a boil and then simmer for 15 minutes. Let it cool. Transfer the mixture to a blender. Pulse until smooth.

Stir in the cheese.

Garnish with the green onion and sour cream before serving.

Nutrition:

Calories 320 Total Fat 19.6g Saturated

Fat 11.9g Cholesterol 54mg Sodium 794mg

Total Carbohydrate 23.2g Dietary Fiber 3.3g
Total Sugars 5.7g Protein 15.1g

Potassium 660mg

Vegetable Soup

Preparation Time: 5 minutes

Cooking Time: 30 minutes

Servings: 6

Ingredients:

2 tablespoons olive oil

1 onion, diced - 2 bell peppers, diced

2 cloves garlic, minced

2 cups green beans, sliced

1 head cauliflower, sliced into florets

1 tablespoon Italian seasoning

8 cups chicken broth

30 oz. diced tomatoes

Salt and pepper to taste

2 dried bay leaves

Directions:

Pour the olive oil in a pot over medium heat.

Sauté the onion and bell peppers for 7 minutes. Add the garlic and cook for 1 minute. Add the rest of the ingredients.

Bring to a boil. Reduce to medium low.

Simmer for 20 minutes.

Nutrition:

Calories 168 Total Fat 7.7g Saturated Fat 1.4g Cholesterol 2mg Sodium 1043mg

Total Carbohydrate 17.1g Dietary Fiber 5.1g Total Sugars 9.2g

Protein 9.9g Potassium 930mg

Mashed Cauliflower with Chives

Preparation Time: 15 minutes

Cooking Time: 25 minutes

Servings: 4

Ingredients:

2 cups chicken broth

2 heads cauliflower, cored and sliced into florets

¼ cup fresh chives, chopped

¼ cup Parmesan cheese, grated

Salt and pepper to taste

Directions:

In a pot over medium heat, pour in the chicken broth. Add the cauliflower. Bring to a boil and then simmer for 20 minutes.

Transfer cauliflower to a blender. Pulse until smooth. Stir in the chives and cheese. Season with salt and pepper.

Nutrition:

Calories 98

Total Fat 3.8g

Saturated Fat 2.2g

Cholesterol 10mg

Sodium 551mg

Total Carbohydrate 8.1g -

Dietary Fiber 3.4g

Total Sugars 3.6g

Protein 9.6g

Potassium 514mg

Garlic Parmesan Zucchini

Preparation Time: 5 minutes

Cooking Time: 20 minutes

Servings: 6

Ingredients:

¼ cup Parmesan cheese

¼ cup mayonnaise

1 clove garlic, minced

Salt to taste

2 zucchinis, sliced

Directions:

Preheat your oven to 400 degrees F.

Combine all the ingredients except the zucchini.

Spread mixture on top of zucchini.

Bake in the oven for 20 minutes.

Nutrition:

Calories 79

Total Fat 5.4g

Saturated Fat 1.8g

Cholesterol 9mg

Sodium 190mg

Total Carbohydrate 5g

Dietary Fiber 0.7g

Total Sugars 1.8g

Protein 3.9g

Potassium 174mg

Cheesy Roasted Broccoli

Preparation Time: 5 minutes

Cooking Time: 10 minutes

Servings: 6

Ingredients:

¼ cup ranch dressing

4 cups broccoli florets

¼ cup heavy whipping cream

½ cup cheddar cheese, shredded

Salt and pepper to taste

Directions:

Preheat your oven to 375 degrees F.

Put all the ingredients in a bowl and mix.

Arrange the broccoli mix on a baking dish.

Bake in the oven for 10 minutes or until tender enough.

Nutrition:

Calories 79

Total Fat 5.2g

Saturated Fat 3.1g

Cholesterol 17mg

Sodium 137mg

Total Carbohydrate 4.8g

Dietary Fiber 1.6g

Total Sugars 1.4g

Protein 4.3g

Potassium 205mg

Stir Fried Green Beans

Preparation Time: 20 minutes

Cooking Time: 10 minutes

Servings: 4

Ingredients:

1 lb. green beans, trimmed and sliced

2 tablespoons peanut oil

2 tablespoons garlic, chopped

½ onion, sliced - Salt to taste

1 tablespoon water

2 tablespoons oyster sauce

Directions:

Add peanut oil to a pan over high heat.

Heat it for 2 minutes.

Add the garlic and onion. Cook for 30 seconds.

Add the beans and season with salt.

Cook for 2 minutes. Pour in the water and cover the pan.

Steam for 5 minutes.

Stir in the oyster sauce and cook for 2 minutes.

Nutrition:

Calories 108 Saturated Fat 1.2g

Cholesterol 0mg

Sodium 102mg Total Carbohydrate 11g

Dietary Fiber 4.3g Total Sugars 2.2g

Protein 2.5g Potassium 275mg

Roasted Asparagus

Preparation Time: 10 minutes

Cooking Time: 20 minutes

Servings: 4

Ingredients:

1 lb. asparagus

1 tablespoon peanut oil

1 teaspoon coconut oil

1 tablespoon soy sauce

1 teaspoon sesame oil

2 teaspoons sesame seeds

Directions:

Preheat your oven to 400 degrees F.

Arrange the asparagus spears on a baking pan. Brush with peanut oil.

Roast for 15 minutes.

While waiting, mix the coconut oil, soy sauce and sesame oil. Brush the asparagus with the mixture and roast for 7 minutes.

Sprinkle with sesame seeds before serving.

Nutrition:

Calories 83

Total Fat 6.5g

Saturated Fat 1.9g

Cholesterol 0mg

Sodium 228mg - Total Carbohydrate 5.1g

Dietary Fiber 2.6g - Total Sugars 2.2g

Protein 3g - Potassium 245mg

CHAPTER 14:

Smoothies Recipes

Matcha Green Juice

Preparation Time: 10 minutes

Cooking time: 0 minutes

Total time: 10 minutes

Servings: 2

Ingredients

5 ounces fresh kale - 2 ounces fresh arugula

¼ cup fresh parsley

4 celery stalks

1 green apple, cored and chopped

1 (1-inch) piece fresh ginger, peeled

1 lemon, peeled

½ teaspoon matcha green tea

Directions

Add all ingredients into a juicer and extract the juice according to the manufacturer's method.

Pour into 2 glasses and serve immediately.

Nutrition:

Calories: 113, Sodium: 22 mg,

Dietary Fibre: 1.2 g, Total Fat: 2.1 g,

Total Carbs: 12.3 g, Protein: 1.3 g.

Celery Juice

Preparation Time: 10 minutes

Cooking time: 0 minutes

Servings: 2

Ingredients

8 celery stalks with leaves - 2 tablespoons fresh ginger, peeled

1 lemon, peeled

½ cup filtered water

Pinch of salt

Instructions

Place all the ingredients in a blender and pulse until well combined. Through a fine mesh strainer, strain the juice and transfer into 2 glasses. Serve immediately.

Nutrition:

Calories: 32, Sodium: 21 mg,

Dietary Fibre: 1.4 g, Total Fat: 1.1 g,

Total Carbs: 1.3 g,

Protein: 1.2 g.

Kale & Orange Juice

Preparation Time: 10 minutes

Cooking time: 0 minutes

Servings: 2

Ingredients

5 large oranges, peeled

2 bunches fresh kale

Directions

Add all ingredients into a juicer and extract the juice according to the manufacturer's method. Pour into 2 glasses and serve immediately.

Nutrition:

Calories: 315,

Sodium: 34 mg,

Dietary Fibre: 1.3 g,

Total Fat: 4.1 g,

Total Carbs: 14.3 g,

Protein: 1.2 g.

Apple & Cucumber Juice

Preparation Time: 10 minutes

Cooking time: 0 minutes

Servings: 2

Ingredients

3 large apples, cored and sliced

2 large cucumbers, sliced

4 celery stalks

1 (1-inch) piece fresh ginger, peeled

1 lemon, peeled

Directions

Add all ingredients into a juicer and extract the juice according to the manufacturer's method.

Pour into 2 glasses and serve immediately.

Nutrition:

Calories: 230, Sodium: 31 mg,

Dietary Fibre: 1.3 g, Total Fat: 2.1 g,

 Total Carbs: 1.3 g,

Protein: 1.2 g.

Lemony Green Juice

Preparation Time: 10 minutes

Cooking time: 0 minutes

Servings: 2

Ingredients

2 large green apples, cored and sliced

4 cups fresh kale leaves

4 tablespoons fresh parsley leaves

1 tablespoon fresh ginger, peeled

1 lemon, peeled

½ cup filtered water

Pinch of salt

Directions

Place all the ingredients in a blender and pulse until well combined. Through a fine mesh strainer, strain the juice and transfer into 2 glasses. Serve immediately.

Nutrition:

Calories: 196, Sodium: 21 mg,

 Dietary Fibre: 1.4 g, Total Fat: 1.1 g

Total Carbs: 1.6 g,

Protein: 1.5 g.

Strawberry Frozen Yogurt

Preparation Time: 10 minutes

Cooking Time: 15 minutes

Servings: 4

Ingredients

15 ounces of plain yogurt

6 ounces of strawberries

Juice of 1 orange

1 tablespoon honey

Directions:

Place the strawberries and orange juice into a food processor or blender and blitz until smooth. Press the mixture through a sieve into a large bowl to remove seeds. Stir in the honey and yogurt. Transfer the mixture to an ice-cream maker and follow the manufacturer's instructions. Alternatively pour the mixture into a container and place in the fridge for 1 hour. Use a fork to whisk it and break up ice crystals and freeze for 2 hours.

Nutrition:

Calories: 238,

Sodium: 33 mg,

Dietary Fibre: 1.4 g,

Total Fat: 1.8 g,

Total Carbs: 12.3 g,

Protein: 1.3 g.

Berry Soy Yogurt Parfait

Preparation Time: 2-4 minutes

Cooking time: 0 minute

Servings: 1

Ingredients

One carton vanilla cultured soy yoghurt

1/4 cup granola (gluten-free)

1 cup berries (you can take strawberries, blueberries, raspberries, blackberries)

Directions

Put half of the yogurt in a glass jar or serving dish. On the top put half of the berries.

Then sprinkle with half of granola

Repeat layers.

Nutrition:

Calories: 244,

Sodium: 33 mg, Dietary Fibre: 1.4 g,

Total Fat: 3.1 g,

Total Carbs: 11.3 g, Protein: 1.4 g.

Orange & Celery Crush

Preparation Time: 10 minutes

Cooking Time: 15 minutes

Servings: 1

Ingredients:

1 carrot, peeled

Stalks of celery

1 orange, peeled

½ teaspoon matcha powder

Juice of 1 lime

Directions:

Place ingredients into a blender with enough water to cover them and blitz until smooth.

Nutrition:

Calories: 150, Sodium: 31 mg,

Dietary Fibre: 1.2 g,

Total Fat: 2.1 g,

Total Carbs: 11.2 g,

Protein: 1.4 g.

Creamy Strawberry & Cherry Smoothie

Preparation Time: 10 minutes

Cooking Time: 15 minutes

Servings: 1

Ingredients:

3½ ounce. Strawberries

3.5 ounce of frozen pitted cherries

1 tablespoon plain full-fat yogurt

6.5 ounce of unsweetened soya milk

Directions:

Place the ingredients into a blender then process until smooth. Serve and enjoy.

 Nutrition:

Calories: 203,

Sodium: 23 mg, Dietary Fibre: 1.4 g,

Total Fat: 3.1 g, Total Carbs: 12.3 g,

Protein: 1.7 g.

Grapefruit & Celery Blast

Preparation Time: 10 minutes

Cooking Time: 15 minutes

Servings: 1

Ingredients

1 grapefruit, peeled

stalks of celery

2-ounce kale

½ teaspoon matcha powder

Directions:

Place ingredients into a blender with water to cover them and blitz until smooth.

Nutrition:

Calories: 129,

Sodium: 24 mg, Dietary Fibre: 1.4 g,

Total Fat: 2.1 g, Total Carbs: 12.1 g,

Protein: 1.2 g.

Walnut & Spiced Apple Tonic

Preparation Time: 10 minutes

Cooking Time: 15 minutes

Servings: 1

Ingredients: ½ teaspoon cinnamon

6 walnuts halves - 1 apple, cored

1 banana - ½ teaspoon matcha powder

Pinch of ground nutmeg

Directions:

Place ingredients into a blender and add sufficient water to cover them. Blitz until smooth and creamy.

Nutrition:

Calories: 124, Sodium: 22 mg,

Dietary Fibre: 1.4 g, Total Fat: 2.1 g,

Total Carbs: 12.3 g, Protein: 1.2 g.

Tropical Chocolate Delight

Preparation Time: 10 minutes

Cooking Time: 15 minutes

Servings: 1

Ingredients

1 mango, peeled & de-stoned

ounce fresh pineapple, chopped

2 ounces of kale

1 ounce of rocket

1 tablespoon 100% cocoa powder or cacao nibs

1 ounce of coconut milk

Direction

Place ingredients into a blender and blitz until smooth. You can add a little water if it seems too thick.

Nutrition:

Calories: 192,

Sodium: 26 mg,

Dietary Fibre: 1.3 g,

Total Fat: 4.1 g,

Total Carbs: 16.6 g,

Protein: 1.6 g.

Conclusion

Keto is a diet that needs to reduce carbohydrates and expanding fats along with the goal of helping the body absorb its own fat stores, each of the most effective. Ketogenic foods are less useful because of their high health and become healthier. Obviously, keto foods have helped specific people get rid of unwanted muscles without the intense cravings that are normal in different weight management programs.

Assuming that it does not go through the negative effects of healthcare difficulties, a keto diet can offer many benefits, especially to reduce weight loss. Basically, eating whole foods is probably the most effective way to eat intensely, basically because it is a supportive strategy.

It is important to note that many studies show that ketogenic weight loss is really difficult to maintain. Therefore, the best advice is to find a consistent way of eating that suits you.

It's okay to try new things, just don't forget first. All of our deals are designed for active moms like you. No injury eats fewer carbohydrates without 3 hours of exercise. Exactly scientific principles that will help you feel the best you've had for years.

Hopefully it has been informative and able to provide you with all the tools you need to deal with Keto Diet.

We've been through definition, adoption, the right mindset, Keto tips and tricks, recipes, overcoming the challenges of the Keto diet and the best fats for Keto diets. You are now familiar with the Keto diet and its recipes for women over 50. You have also learned that you can change your diet and lose weight.

I want to leave you with a few words of advice and motivation. The first time you start this diet it may seem easy because of the motivation. Motivation tends to die after the first two days and then you let go of discipline. It can start to feel self-sacrificing when your friends or family eat pizza and you're stuck eating a salad. You will guess your new option over and over and wonder if you are doing the right thing. This is all perfectly normal. I cried because I thought it was so unfair that I couldn't eat cake or pizza like everyone else, but I always went out and realized the reality. Actually, she could eat anything, but she couldn't lose the weight she wanted if she did. I really don't want what they have, right now it seems like I'm missing it, but actually, no. The following thing is, Keto isn't for everyone, but it's likely for you if you've already reached it! Don't try to persuade your spouse and children to join you if they're not ready, or pressure your best friends. Do it yourself. The best way to change others is to change yourself and let your success be contagious and desirable for others to see. Finally, don't be antisocial because you are afraid of food and being around others. Get out, have fun, but before you go, always GET READY.

THE BEST!